BOOK OF WORDS

OF

WORDS

17,000 Words Selected by Vowels and Diphthongs

by Valeda Blockcolsky, M.S., CCC-SLP

Communication Skill Builders

3830 E. Bellevue/P.O. Box 42050
Tucson, Arizona 85733
(602) 323-7500

© 1990 by

Communication
Skill Builders, Inc.
3830 E. Bellevue/P.O. Box 42050
Tucson, Arizona 85733
(602) 323-7500

ISBN 0-88450-327-5   Catalog No. 7627

10 9 8 7 6 5 4 3 2
Printed in the United States of America

About the Author

Valeda Blockcolsky, M.S., CCC-SLP, is a cofounder of Communication Skill Builders and has coauthored several educational products, including *Peel & Put*® and *40,000 Selected Words*. She is currently employed by the Fairbanks North Star Borough School District in Fairbanks, Alaska, as a speech-language pathologist.

She received the B.S. degree in Speech Pathology from Kansas State University and the M.S. degree in Speech Pathology from Southern Illinois University. She holds the Certificate of Clinical Competence from ASHA and has been an active member of the American Speech-Language-Hearing Association since 1969.

Contents

O /ɔ/ (ostrich)
Initial

Final

OI /ɔɪ/ (oil)
Initial

Final

Introduction

Book of Words: 17,000 Words Selected by Vowels and Diphthongs is a comprehensive resource containing word lists organized by vowel and diphthong sounds, r-colored vowels, and rhyming words. The word lists contain a wide range of vocabulary levels that can be selected for any audience or age level. The unique lists of r-colored vowels are an especially useful feature.

Speech-language pathologists will find these lists invaluable in selecting precise phonemes for speech therapy. This text will be an excellent resource for application with articulation disorders, apraxia, dysarthria, hearing impairments, nasality, or voice disorders. Classroom teachers can use this reference to teach vowel-consonant combinations, spelling patterns, poetry, and rhyming words. English as a second language students will find this text especially helpful in perfecting correct pronunciation. Finally, writers and poets can use this book as a rhyming dictionary to locate words that fit particular meters or rhyme schemes.

Book of Words lists one-syllable and two-syllable words for 32 different vowel and diphthong sounds. The table of contents identifies each vowel by orthographic symbol followed by a sample word in parentheses. A table immediately following the introduction lists, for each sound, the orthographic symbol used in this book, the International Phonetic Alphabet Symbol, and the dictionary symbol used to represent the sound. Examples of each sound in initial, medial, and final position are also provided.

The book is divided into two sections: The first section contains 17 different sounds, beginning with vowels that are represented with the letter A, followed by E, I, O, and U. The second section contains 15 different r-colored vowels. Each vowel in this section is immediately followed by an R, which affects how it is pronounced. Included in this section are two-syllable words that end in ER.

For each vowel sound, there are two sets of lists. The first set includes one- and two-syllable words organized by consonant-vowel combinations. The target vowel is always the first vowel sound that occurs in the word. The second list is organized by final sounds. It consists of one-syllable words and final ER words, organized for rhyming. Words were selected for inclusion based on the following general criteria:

1. The words were selected from the second edition of the *Random House Unabridged Dictionary* and *Webster's Third New International Dictionary*.

2. Only words that are listed as separate entries in the dictionary are included in the word lists.

3. If there are two adjacent vowels in the word (*dial, hour*), the first vowel determines placement.

4. All proper names have been omitted.

5. Many words that have derogatory, offensive, or demeaning meanings have been omitted. However, many common words with double meanings are listed. It is assumed that the clinician will select words that are appropriate to the client and context.

6. In general, words referring to drugs, alcohol, or violence have not been included. Also, words that are sexist or sexually biased have been omitted (for example, *bellboy* as opposed to *bellhop*.)

7. Words with alternative accepted pronunciations are listed in more than one list.

Table 1: Symbols corresponding to vowel sounds included in this manual

Orthographic Symbol	IPA Symbol	Dictionary Symbol*	Sample Words Initial	Medial	Final
A	/e/	ā	age	date	bay
A	/æ/	a	apple	bag	baa
A	/ɑ/	ä	almond	balm	spa
A	/ə/	ə	award	canoe	tuba
E	/i/	ē	eagle	feet	sea
E	/ɛ/	e	egg	jet	
I	/aɪ/	ī	island	tiger	pie
I	/ɪ/	i	igloo	fish	
O	/o/	ō	ocean	hotel	toe
O	/ɒ/	o	olive	box	
O	/ɔ/	ô	ostrich	dog	saw
OI	/ɔɪ/	oi	oil	coin	boy
OU	/aʊ/	ou	owl	south	cow
U	/u/	o͞o	ooze	food	shoe
YU	/ju/	yo͞o	you	bugle	view
U	/ʊ/	o͝o	umlaut	foot	
U	/ʌ/	u	onion	sun	
AIR	/ɛər/	âr	airplane	dairy	bear
AR	/ær/	ar	arrow	parrot	
AR	/ɑr/	är	arm	card	car
AR	/ər/	ər	arrive	giraffe	
ER	/ir/	ēr	ear	zero	deer
ER	/ɛr/	er	error	berry	
IR	/aɪər/	īər	ire	fireplace	tire
IR	/aɪr/	īr	iris	pirate	
IR	/ɪr/	ir	erase	mirror	
OR	/ɔr/, /or/	ôr, ōr	oar	board	door
OUR	/aʊr/	ouər	our	sourness	hour
UR	/ʊr/	o͝or		tourist	sure
YUR	/jʊr/	yo͝or	your	mural	cure
UR	/ɝ/	ûr	earth	bird	bur
ER	/ɚ/	ər		percent	teacher

*Symbols used in the *Random House Dictionary of the English Language*.

A /e/

A /e/ — one syllable

ace	aide	ape
ache	ail	ate
age	aim	eight
aid	aitch	eighth

A /e/ — two syllables

able	aimer	éclair
ably	aimless	eighteen
acorn	ancient	eighteenth
acre	angel	eightfold
aged	apex	eighty
ageless	aphid	emir
agent	apish	etude
ailment	apron	_____

BA /be/ — one syllable

babe	bale	bathe
bait	bane	bay
baize	base	beige
bake	baste	_____

BA /be/ — two syllables

baby	bake-off	basil
bacon	baler	basin
bagel	basal	basis
bailiff	baseball	bated
bailout	basement	bather
baker	basic	bathing

1

CHA /tʃe/ —one syllable

chafe	change	_____
chain	chase	

CHA /tʃe/ —two syllables

chafer	chamber	_____
chainstitch	changeless	_____
chainwork	chasten	_____

DA /de/ —one syllable

dale	day	_____
dame	daze	_____
date	deign	_____

DA /de/ —two syllables

daily	dateline	daytime
dainty	dative	daywork
dais	daybreak	debut
daisy	daydream	_____
dated	daylight	_____

FA /fe/ —one syllable

face	fame	fete
fade	famed	phase
fail	fate	_____
faint	faze	_____
faith	feign	_____
fake	feint	_____

FA /fe/ —two syllables

fable	fade-out	famous
faceless	failing	fatal
face-lift	failure	favor
face-off	fainter	favored
facial	faintly	_____
facing	faithful	_____
faded	faker	_____

A

GA /ge/ —one syllable

gain	gape	gaze
gait	gate	_____
gale	gauge	_____
game	gave	_____

GA /ge/ —two syllables

gable	gainsay	gater
gabled	gaiter	gateway
gaily	gala	_____
gainer	gamely	_____
gainful	gatepost	_____

HA /he/ —one syllable

hail	hay	_____
haste	haze	_____
hate	hey	_____

HA /he/ —two syllables

halo	hater	haystack
hasten	haven	hazel
hasty	hayloft	hazy
hateful	hayride	_____

JA /dʒe/ —one syllable

jade	_____	_____
jail	_____	_____
jay	_____	_____

JA /dʒe/ —two syllables

jaded	jailer	_____
jailbird	jaywalk	_____

KA /ke/ —one syllable

cage	cape	_____
cake	case	_____
came	cave	_____
cane	kale	_____

KA /kē/—two syllables

cable	calyx	casement
cadence	cambric	casework
cagey	canine	cater
cakewalk	caper	chaos
caliph	capon	_____
calix	caseload	_____

LA /lē/—one syllable

lace	lake	lay
laced	lame	laze
lade	lane	lei
laid	late	_____
lain	lathe	_____

LA /lē/—two syllables

label	lady	latex
labile	lamely	layer
labor	lameness	layman
lacing	laser	layoff
lacy	latent	layout
laden	later	lazy
ladle	latest	_____

MA /mē/—one syllable

mace	main	mange
made	maize	mate
maid	make	may
mail	male	maze
maim	mane	_____

MA /mē/—two syllables

maiden	mainland	makeshift
mailbag	mainsail	makeup
mailbox	maintain	making
mailer	major	maleness
mailing	maker	manger

maple	mayfly	_____
matrix	mayor	_____
matron	melee	_____
maybe	mesa	_____

A

NA /ne/ —one syllable

nail	nave	_____
name	nay	_____
nape	neigh	_____

NA /ne/ —two syllables

nabob	namesake	native
nadir	nametag	nature
nailbrush	nasal	naval
nameless	nascent	navel
namely	natal	navy
nameplate	nation	neighbor

PA /pe/ —one syllable

pace	pain	paste
page	paint	pave
paid	pale	pay
pail	pane	_____

PA /pe/ —two syllables

pacer	paisley	paving
pagan	paling	paycheck
pageboy	papal	payday
pager	paper	payer
paging	pasteboard	payment
pailful	paste-up	payoff
painful	pastry	payroll
painless	pasty	peso
paintbrush	patience	_____
painted	patient	_____
painter	patron	_____
painting	pavement	_____

RA /re/ —one syllable

race	rake	reign
rage	range	rein
raid	rate	_____
rail	rave	_____
rain	ray	_____
raise	raze	_____

RA /re/ —two syllables

rabies	railway	rater
racecourse	raiment	rating
raceway	rainbow	ratio
racial	raincoat	ration
racing	raindrop	raven
racy	rainfall	razor
radar	rainy	regime
radon	raisin	reindeer
raging	raising	_____
raider	raker	_____
railing	ramose	_____
railroad	ranger	_____

SA /se/ —one syllable

safe	sake	save
sage	sale	say
sail	same	_____
saint	sane	_____

SA /se/ —two syllables

saber	sailcloth	sameness
sable	sailfish	saving
sacred	sailing	savior
safeguard	sailor	savor
safety	saintly	saying
sagebrush	salesclerk	_____
sagely	salesroom	_____
sailboat	saline	_____

A

SHA /ʃe/ —one syllable
chaise	shale	shave
shade	shame	_____
shake	shape	_____

SHA /ʃe/ —two syllables
shading	shameful	shaving
shady	shapeless	_____
shaker	shapely	_____
shake-up	shaven	_____
shaky	shaver	_____

TA /te/ —one syllable
tail	tale	taste
taint	tame	_____
take	tape	_____

TA /te/ —two syllables
table	takeoff	tasteless
tabling	takeout	taster
tabor	taker	tasty
tailback	taking	_____
tailgate	tamely	_____
tailing	tameness	_____
tailor	tamer	_____
tailpipe	taper	_____
tailspin	tapir	_____
tailwind	tasteful	_____

THA /ðe/ —one syllable
they	they'll	_____
they'd	they've	_____

VA /ve/ —one syllable
vague	vane	vein
vail	vase	_____
vain	veil	_____

VA /ve/ —two syllables

vacant	vainly	veinlet
vacate	vainness	veinule
vagrant	valence	_____
vaguely	valent	_____
vagueness	vapor	_____
vagus	veiling	_____

WA /we/ —one syllable

wade	wake	weight
wage	wane	_____
wail	waste	_____
waist	wave	_____
wait	way	_____
waive	weigh	_____

WA /we/ —two syllables

wader	waken	wayward
wafer	wastage	weightless
wager	wasteful	weighty
waistband	waveless	_____
waiter	waver	_____
waiting	wavy	_____
waitress	waylay	_____
waiver	way-out	_____
wakeful	wayside	_____

WHA /ʍe/ —one syllable

whale	_____	_____
whey	_____	_____

WHA /ʍe/ —two syllables

whaleboat	whaler	_____
whalebone	whaling	_____

ZA /ze/ —two syllables

zany	_____	_____

A /e/—final

bay	lei	stay
bray	may	stray
clay	nay	sway
day	pay	they
dray	play	tray
flay	pray	way
fray	prey	weigh
gray	ray	whey
hay	say	_____
hey	sleigh	_____
jay	splay	_____
lay	spray	_____

AB /eb/—final
babe   _____   _____

AD /ed/—final

aid	made	trade
aide	maid	wade
blade	paid	weighed
braid	raid	_____
fade	shade	_____
glade	spade	_____
grade	staid	_____
jade	stayed	_____
lade	suede	_____
laid	they'd	_____

AF /ef/—final

chafe	_____	_____
safe	_____	_____
waif	_____	_____

AG /eg/—final

plague	_____	_____
vague	_____	_____

AJ /edʒ/ —final

age	page	stage
cage	rage	wage
gauge	sage	_____

ANJ /endʒ/ —final

change	mange	strange
grange	range	_____

AK /ek/ —final

ache	flake	shake
bake	hake	slake
brake	lake	snake
break	make	stake
cake	quake	steak
drake	rake	take
fake	sake	wake

AL /el/ —final

ail	mail	swale
bail	male	tail
bale	nail	tale
dale	pail	they'll
fail	pale	trail
flail	quail	vail
frail	rail	veil
gale	sail	wail
grail	sale	whale
hail	scale	_____
hale	shale	_____
jail	snail	_____
kale	stale	_____

AM /em/ —final

aim	claim	flame
blame	dame	frame
came	fame	game

lame	same	_____
maim	shame	_____
name	tame	_____

A

AN /en/ —final

bane	lane	stain
brain	main	strain
cane	mane	swain
chain	pain	train
crane	pane	vain
deign	plain	vane
drain	plane	vein
feign	rain	wane
gain	reign	_____
grain	sane	_____
lain	sprain	_____

AP /ep/ —final

ape	grape	tape
cape	nape	_____
crepe	scape	_____
drape	scrape	_____
gape	shape	_____

AS /es/ —final

ace	grace	space
base	lace	trace
brace	mace	vase
case	pace	_____
chase	place	_____
face	race	_____

APS /eps/ —final

capes	grapes	tapes
crepes	napes	traipse
drapes	scrapes	_____
gapes	shapes	_____

AT /et/ —final

ate	late	strait
bait	mate	trait
crate	pate	wait
date	plait	weight
eight	plate	_____
fate	prate	_____
freight	rate	_____
gait	skate	_____
gate	slate	_____
grate	spate	_____
great	state	_____
hate	straight	_____

ANT /ent/ —final

faint	quaint	taint
paint	saint	_____

AST /est/ —final

aced	graced	taste
based	haste	traced
baste	laced	waist
braced	paced	waste
cased	paste	_____
chased	placed	_____
faced	raced	_____

ATH /eð/ —final

bathe	lathe	scathe

ATH /eθ/ —final

faith	_____	_____

ATTH /etθ/

eighth	_____	_____

AV /ev/—final

brave	nave	stave
cave	pave	they've
crave	rave	waive
gave	save	wave
grave	shave	_____
knave	slave	_____

AZ /ez/—final

baize	haze	raise
bays	jays	rays
blaze	laze	raze
braise	leis	sprays
brays	maize	stays
chaise	maze	strays
craze	pays	sways
days	phase	trays
daze	phrase	ways
faze	plays	weighs
flays	praise	_____
gaze	prays	_____
glaze	preys	_____

AZH /eʒ/—final

beige	_____	_____

A /æ/

A /æ/ — one syllable

act	an	ask
add	and	asp
adz	ant	at
alp	apt	aunt
am	as	ax
amp	ash	

A /æ/ — two syllables

abbey	admire	amply
abbot	admit	anchor
abhor	advance	android
abject	advent	anger
absent	adverb	angle
accent	adverse	angler
accept	advice	angry
access	advise	anise
acme	after	ankle
acne	agate	anklet
acrid	agile	annex
acting	album	anode
action	alcove	answer
active	alley	ante
actor	alloy	anthem
actress	ally	anthill
adage	aloe	antic
addend	alpine	antique
adder	amber	antler
addle	amble	anvil
adhere	ampere	anxious
ad-lib	ample	apple

A

aptly	aster	axis
ascot	asthma	axle
ashen	astral	axon
asking	athlete	azure
aspect	atlas	_____
aspen	atoll	_____
asphalt	atom	_____
aspic	attic	_____
asset	avid	_____

BA /bæ/ —one syllable

baa	ban	bass
back	band	bat
bad	bang	batch
badge	bank	bath
bag	bash	_____
bam	bask	_____

BA /bæ/ —two syllables

babble	backtrack	bamboo
baboon	backup	bandage
backache	backward	bandbox
backbend	backyard	banded
backbone	badger	bandstand
backcourt	badly	bandy
backdrop	badness	banger
backer	baffle	bangle
backfield	bagful	banish
backfire	baggage	banjo
background	bagger	banker
backhoe	baggy	banner
backing	bagpipe	banquet
backlog	balance	bantam
backpack	ballad	banter
backstage	ballast	banyan
backstop	ballet	bashful
backstroke	ballot	basil

basket	bathroom	batting
basset	bathtub	battle
bassoon	batten	_____
bathrobe	batter	_____

CHA /tʃæ/—one syllable

chaff	chant	chat
champ	chap	_____
chance	chaps	_____

CHA /tʃæ/—two syllables

chalice	chanter	chattel
challenge	chapel	chatter
chancel	chaplain	chatty
chancy	chapter	_____
channel	chassis	_____

DA /dæ/—one syllable

dab	damp	dap
dad	dance	dash
dam	dank	_____

DA /dæ/—two syllables

dabble	dampness	dapper
dabbler	damsel	dapple
daddy	dancer	dashboard
dagger	dander	dasher
dally	dandle	dashing
damage	dandruff	dazzle
damask	dandy	_____
dampen	dangle	_____
damper	dankness	_____

FA /fæ/—one syllable

fact	fang	fat
fad	fanged	fax
fan	fast	_____

FA /fæ/—two syllables

fabric	falcon	fastback
facet	famine	fasten
facile	famish	fathom
faction	fancy	fatten
factor	fanfare	fatter
faddish	fashion	phantom

GA /gæ/—one syllable

gab	gag	gap
gad	gal	gas
gaff	gam	gash
gaffe	gang	gasp

GA /gæ/—two syllables

gabble	gambit	gangway
gabby	gamble	gasket
gadget	gambler	gastric
gallant	gamma	gather
galley	gamut	gavel
gallon	gander	_____
gallop	gangly	_____

HA /hæ/—one syllable

hack	hand	hat
had	hang	hatch
haft	hank	hath
half	has	have
halve	hash	_____
ham	hasp	_____

HA /hæ/—two syllables

habit	haddock	half-hour
hacker	hadn't	half-life
hackle	haggard	half-moon
hackney	haggle	halfway
hacksaw	halfback	halide

A

hallow	handmade	hasn't
hamlet	hand-off	hassle
hammer	handout	hassock
hammock	handsaw	hatbox
hamper	handshake	hatchet
hamster	handsome	hatching
handbag	handspring	hatless
handball	handstand	hatpin
handbill	handwork	hatrack
handbook	handwrite	hatter
handcart	handy	havoc
handclasp	hanger	hazard
handcraft	hangout	_____
handcuff	hansom	_____
handed	hapless	_____
handful	happen	_____
handle	happy	_____

JA /dʒæ/—one syllable

jab	jag	jazz
jack	jam	_____
jacks	jamb	_____

JA /dʒæ/—two syllables

jabber	jackpot	jasper
jackal	jagged	jazzy
jackdaw	jaguar	_____
jacket	jangle	_____
jackknife	jasmine	_____

KA /kæ/—one syllable

cab	camp	cast
cache	can	caste
cad	can't	cat
cadge	cant	catch
calf	cap	_____
cam	cash	_____

A

KA /kæ/ —two syllables

cabbage	candid	casting
cabby	candle	castle
cabin	candy	castoff
cachet	canner	castor
cackle	canning	catcher
cactus	cannon	catching
caddie	canny	catchy
cadger	canon	catfish
café	canteen	catlike
caffeine	canter	catnap
caftan	canvas	cattail
callous	canyon	cattle
callow	capful	catwalk
callus	capsize	cavern
camel	capsule	chasm
campaign	captain	_____
camper	caption	_____
campfire	captive	_____
campground	captor	_____
camphor	capture	_____
campout	cascade	_____
campsite	cashew	_____
campstool	cashier	_____
campus	cashmere	_____
cancan	casket	_____
cancel	cassock	_____
cancer	caster	_____

LA /læ/ —one syllable

lab	land	latch
lack	lank	laugh
lad	lap	lax
lag	lapse	_____
lamb	lash	_____
lamp	lass	_____
lance	last	_____

LA /læ/—two syllables

lackey	landfill	lasso
lacking	landform	lasting
lacquer	landing	lastly
lactic	landlord	latching
lactose	landmark	lather
ladder	landmass	latter
laggard	landscape	lattice
lagging	landslide	laughing
lambkin	language	laughter
lambskin	languid	lavish
lampoon	lantern	laxly
lamprey	lanyard	_____
lancer	lapboard	_____
landed	lapis	_____

MA /mæ/—one syllable

ma'am	mash	match
mad	mask	math
mag	masque	max
man	mass	_____
manse	mast	_____
map	mat	_____

MA /mæ/—two syllables

macro	mallard	manner
madam	mallet	manor
madcap	mammal	mansion
madness	mammoth	mantel
maggot	manage	mantis
magic	mandate	mantle
magma	mangle	mapping
magnate	mango	mascot
magnet	manhole	masher
magnum	manhood	masking
magpie	manic	massive
malice	manly	master

mastoid	matted	maxim
matchbook	matter	
matchbox	matting	
matching	mattress	
matchwood	maxi	

NA /næ/—one syllable

gnash	nab	natch
gnat	nag	
knack	nap	

NA /næ/—two syllables

knapsack	napper	natty
nagger	napping	
napkin	nascent	

PA /pæ/—one syllable

pack	pant	patch
pact	pants	path
pad	pap	
pal	pass	
pan	past	
pang	pat	

PA /pæ/—two syllables

package	palette	pantry
packet	pallet	pantsuit
packing	pallid	panty
packsack	pallor	papoose
padding	pamper	passage
paddle	pamphlet	passbook
paddock	pancake	passing
paddy	panda	passive
padlock	panel	passkey
pageant	panic	passport
palace	pansy	password
palate	panther	pastel

pastime	patchy	pattern
pastor	patent	patty
pasture	pathway	_____
patchwork	patter	_____

RA /ræ/—one syllable

rack	ranch	rasp
rad	rang	rat
raft	rank	razz
rag	rant	wrack
ram	rap	wrap
ramp	rapt	wrath
ran	rash	_____

RA /ræ/—two syllables

rabbi	ramble	rapture
rabbit	rampage	rascal
rabble	rampant	rashly
rabid	rampart	rashness
raccoon	rancher	raspy
racket	rancid	ratchet
radish	random	rather
raffle	rankle	ration
rafter	rankness	rattan
rafting	ransack	rattle
ragged	rapid	ravage
ragout	rapids	ravel
ragtime	rappel	ravish
ragtop	rapping	wrangle
ragweed	rapport	wrapper
rally	raptness	wrapping

SA /sæ/—one syllable

sack	sand	sash
sad	sang	sass
sag	sank	sat
salve	sap	sax

A

SA /sæ/—two syllables

sachet	salvo	sapphire
sackful	sampan	sappy
sadden	sample	sassy
saddle	sandal	satchel
saddler	sandbag	sateen
sadness	sandbox	satin
saffron	sandbur	satire
saggy	sanded	savage
salad	sander	savvy
sallow	sandfish	_____
sally	sandstone	_____
salmon	sandstorm	_____
salvage	sandwich	_____
salver	sapling	_____

SHA /ʃæ/—one syllable

shack	shall	shank
shad	shalt	_____
shaft	sham	_____
shag	shan't	_____

SHA /ʃæ/—two syllables

chalet	shaggy	shampoo
chamois	shallot	shamrock
chateau	shallow	shanty
shabby	shamble	shatter
shackle	shambles	_____
shadow	shammer	_____

TA /tæ/—one syllable

tab	tan	tat
tack	tang	tax
tact	tank	_____
tad	tap	_____
tag	taps	_____
tamp	task	_____

TA /tæ/—two syllables

tabby	talcum	tanker
tablet	talent	tanner
tabloid	tallow	tanning
tacit	tally	tapper
tackle	talon	tapping
tacky	tambour	taproot
tactful	tamper	tassel
tactic	tandem	tattoo
tactile	tangent	tatter
tadpole	tangle	tattered
taffy	tango	tattle
tagboard	tangy	taxi

THA /ðæ/—one syllable

than	that	that's

THA /ðæ/—two syllables

that'll	_____	_____

THA /θæ/—one syllable

thank	_____	_____
thatch	_____	_____

THA /θæ/—two syllables

thankful	thank-you	thatching
thankless	thatcher	_____

VA /væ/—one syllable

valve	vang	vat
van	vast	_____

VA /væ/—two syllables

vaccine	valid	valued
vacuum	valley	vampire
valet	valor	vandal
valiant	value	vanguard

A

vanish	vapid	vastness
vanquish	vassal	_____
vantage	vastly	_____

WA /wæ/—one syllable

waft	_____	_____
wag	_____	_____
wax	_____	_____

WA /wæ/—two syllables

wacky	wangle	waxy
wafture	waxen	_____
waggle	waxer	_____
wagon	waxworks	_____

WHA /ʍæ/—one syllable

whack	_____	_____
wham	_____	_____
whang	_____	_____

WHA /ʍæ/—two syllables

whacker	whammo	_____
whacking	whammy	_____

YA /jæ/—one syllable

yak	yank	_____
yam	yap	_____

YA /jæ/—two syllables

yammer	yapping	_____

ZA /zæ/—one syllable

zag	zap	_____

ZA /zæ/—two syllables

zander	zapping	_____
zapper	zappy	_____

A /æ/—final
baa

AB /æb/—final

blab	flab	nab
cab	gab	scab
crab	grab	slab
dab	jab	tab
drab	lab	_____

ACH /ætʃ/—final

batch	match	snatch
catch	natch	thatch
hatch	patch	_____
latch	scratch	_____

ANCH /æntʃ/—final

blanch	branch	ranch

AD /æd/—final

add	fad	pad
bad	gad	plaid
brad	glad	rad
cad	had	sad
clad	lad	shad
dad	mad	tad

AND /ænd/—final

and	gland	rand
band	grand	sand
bland	hand	stand
brand	land	strand

AF /æf/—final

calf	gaffe	laugh
chaff	graph	quaff
gaff	half	staff

A

AG /æg/ — final

bag	lag	slag
brag	mag	snag
crag	nag	stag
drag	rag	swag
flag	sag	tag
gag	scrag	wag
jag	shag	zag

AJ /ædʒ/ — final

badge	cadge	_____

AK /æk/ — final

back	pack	snack
black	plaque	stack
clack	quack	tack
flack	rack	track
hack	sack	whack
jack	shack	wrack
knack	slack	yak
lack	smack	_____

ASK /æsk/ — final

ask	cask	task
bask	mask	_____

AL /æl/ — final

pal	shall	_____

ALK /ælk/ — final

talc	_____	_____

AM /æm/ — final

am	cram	ham
bam	dam	jam
cam	dram	lamb
clam	gram	ma'am

pram	slam	_____
ram	swam	_____
scam	tram	_____
scram	wham	_____
sham	yam	_____

AN /æn/ —final

an	man	than
ban	pan	van
bran	plan	_____
can	ran	_____
clan	scan	_____
fan	span	_____
flan	tan	_____

ANG /æŋ/ —final

bang	pang	tang
clang	rang	twang
fang	sang	whang
gang	slang	_____
hang	sprang	_____

ANK /æŋk/ —final

bank	frank	spank
blank	hank	stank
clank	lank	swank
crank	plank	tank
dank	prank	thank
drank	rank	yank
flank	sank	_____
franc	shank	_____

AP /æp/ —final

cap	flap	nap
chap	gap	rap
clap	lap	sap
dap	map	scrap

A

slap	trap	_____
snap	wrap	_____
strap	yap	_____
tap	zap	_____

ALP /ælp/ —final

alp	scalp	_____

AMP /æmp/ —final

amp	cramp	scamp
camp	damp	stamp
champ	lamp	tamp
clamp	ramp	tramp

ASP /æsp/ —final

asp	gasp	hasp
clasp	grasp	rasp

AS /æs/ —final

bass	gas	mass
brass	glass	pass
class	grass	sass
crass	lass	_____

AKS /æks/ —final

ax	packs	snacks
backs	racks	stacks
cracks	sacks	tacks
fax	sax	tax
flax	shacks	tracks
jacks	slacks	wax
lax	smacks	whacks

ANS /æns/ —final

chance	lance	stance
dance	manse	_____
glance	prance	_____

ASH /æʃ/—final

ash	gash	splash
bash	gnash	stash
brash	hash	thrash
cache	lash	trash
cash	mash	_____
clash	rash	_____
crash	sash	_____
dash	slash	_____
flash	smash	_____

AT /æt/—final

at	hat	splat
bat	mat	sprat
brat	pat	stat
cat	plait	tat
chat	rat	that
drat	sat	vat
fat	scat	_____
flat	slat	_____
gnat	spat	_____

AFT /æft/—final

aft	graphed	staffed
craft	haft	waft
daft	laughed	_____
draft	raft	_____
graft	shaft	

AKT /ækt/—final

act	jacked	tacked
backed	lacked	tact
blacked	packed	tracked
clacked	pact	tract
cracked	quacked	whacked
fact	smacked	wracked
hacked	snacked	_____

A

ANT /ænt/—final

ant	chant	rant
aunt	grant	scant
can't	pant	slant
cant	plant	_____

APT /æpt/—final

apt	napped	tapped
capped	rapped	trapped
chapped	rapt	wrapped
clapped	scrapped	yapped
flapped	slapped	zapped
lapped	snapped	_____
mapped	strapped	_____

AST /æst/—final

blast	gassed	passed
cast	hast	past
caste	last	sassed
fast	mast	vast

ATH /æθ/—final

bath	math	wrath
hath	path	_____

AV /æv/—final

calve	have	_____
halve	salve	_____

ALV /ælv/—final

valve	_____	_____

AZ /æz/—final

as	has	razz
baas	jazz	_____

A /ɑ/

A /ɑ/ —one syllable

aah	alms	_____
ah	aunt	_____

A /ɑ/ —two syllables

achoo	almsman	entente
aha	amen	entrée
ahu	aqua	_____
alba	auntie	_____
almond	encore	_____

BA /bɑ/ —one syllable

baa	balm	_____

BA /bɑ/ —two syllables

balmy	_____	_____

CHA /tʃɑ/ —two syllables

cha-cha	_____	_____

DA /dɑ/ —two syllables

dachshund	dada	dahlia

FA /fɑ/ —one syllable

fa	_____	_____

FA /fɑ/ —two syllables

father	_____	_____

GA /gɑ/ —two syllables

gaga	_____	_____

A

HA /hɑ/—one syllable
hah   halve   _____

HA /hɑ/—two syllables
ha-ha   _____   _____

JA /dʒɑ/—one syllable
jaunt   _____   _____

JA /dʒɑ/—two syllables
jaunty   _____   _____

KA /kɑ/—one syllable
calf   calm   _____

KA /kɑ/—two syllables
calmly   kaput   _____
calmness   kava   _____

LA /lɑ/—one syllable
la   lat   launch

LA /lɑ/—two syllables
lava   llama   llano

MA /mɑ/—one syllable
ma   mach   malm

MA /mɑ/—two syllables
macho   mama   mambo
mahjongg   mamba   matzo

NA /nɑ/—two syllables
nachos   naive   _____

PA /pɑ/—one syllable
pa   palm   palmed

PA /pɑ/—two syllables

padre	palmy	pâté
palmar	papa	_____
palmist	pasta	_____

RA /rɑ/—two syllables

rah-rah	rajah	_____

SA /sɑ/—one syllable

psalm	_____	_____

SA /sɑ/—two syllables

psalmist	saga	salsa
sabra	sahib	_____

SHA /ʃɑ/—one syllable

shah	_____	_____

SHA /ʃɑ/—two syllables

shadoof	shaman	_____
shalom	shammes	_____

TA /tɑ/—two syllables

tabla	tala	thalweg
taco	tallith	_____

WA /wɑ/—one syllable

waft	_____	_____

WA /wɑ/—two syllables

waftage	wafture	wahoo

YA /jɑ/—two syllables

yahoo	_____	_____

ZHA /ʒɑ/—two syllables

genre	_____	_____

A /ɑ/—final

aah	fa	pa
ah	hah	schwa
baa	la	shah
blah	ma	spa

ANCH /ɑntʃ/—final

staunch   _____   _____

AM /ɑm/—final

balm	palm	qualm
calm	psalm	_____

AT /ɑt/—final

yacht   _____   _____

AV /ɑv/—final

halve   suave   _____

A

A /ə/

A /ə/—two syllables

aback	accused	afire
abase	achieve	aflame
abash	acquaint	afloat
abate	acquire	afoot
abeam	acquit	afoul
abed	across	afraid
abet	acute	afresh
abide	adapt	again
ablaze	address	against
abloom	adduce	agape
aboard	adept	agaze
abode	adjoin	aghast
abound	adjourn	agleam
about	adjure	aglow
above	adjust	ago
abreast	ado	agog
abridge	adopt	agree
abroad	adore	agreed
abrupt	adorn	aground
abuse	adrift	ahead
abut	adroit	ahem
abuzz	adult	ahold
abyss	afar	ahoy
acclaim	affair	ajar
accord	affect	akin
accost	affirm	alack
account	affix	alarm
accrue	afflict	alas
accursed	afford	alert
accuse	afield	alight

align	apiece	astray
alike	aplomb	astride
alive	appall	astute
allay	appeal	athirst
allege	appear	atilt
allied	appease	atone
allot	append	atop
allow	applaud	attach
allude	applause	attack
allure	apply	attain
ally	appoint	attempt
aloft	appraise	attend
alone	apprise	attest
along	approach	attire
aloof	approve	attract
aloud	ascend	attune
amass	ascent	avail
amaze	ascribe	avenge
amend	ashamed	aver
amid	ashore	averse
amidst	aside	avert
amiss	askance	avoid
among	askew	await
amongst	aslant	awake
amount	asleep	award
amuse	aspire	aware
amused	assail	awash
anew	assent	away
anneal	assert	aweigh
annex	assign	awhile
announce	assist	awhirl
annoy	assort	awoke
annul	assuage	emir
anoint	assume	object
anon	assure	oblige
apace	astir	oblique
apart	astound	obscure

observe	occlude	oppose
obsess	occult	oppress
obstruct	occur	upon
obtain	o'clock	_____
obtrude	offend	_____
obtuse	offense	_____

BA /bə/—two syllables
baleen	bassoon	bazaar
balloon	batik	buffet
basalt	baton	buffoon

DA /də/—two syllables
| debris | depute | _____ |
| denier | devoir | _____ |

FA /fə/—two syllables
| facade | fakir | fatigued |
| fainaigue | fatigue | _____ |

GA /gə/—two syllables
gadroon	galosh	gazelle
galloon	galumph	gazette
galoot	gavage	gestalt
galore	gavotte	guffaw

HA /hə/—two syllables
| hallo | hamal | _____ |
| halloo | huzzah | _____ |

KA /kə/—two syllables
cabal	cajole	canoe
caboose	calash	capot
cadelle	calotte	capote
cadet	camise	caprice
café	canal	cassette
cahoot	canard	cocoon

A

collage	conceit	consist
collapse	conceive	console
collate	concent	conspire
collect	concern	consult
collide	concerned	consume
collude	concise	contain
cologne	conclude	contempt
combat	concur	contend
combine	condemn	content
combined	condense	contest
combust	condensed	contort
command	condole	contract
commence	condone	contrast
commend	conduce	contrite
commit	confect	contrive
commune	confer	control
commute	confess	convene
compact	confide	converge
compare	confine	converse
compart	confined	convert
compeer	confirm	convey
compel	confirmed	convict
compete	conflict	convince
compile	conform	kabob
complain	confront	kaboom
complaint	confuse	kazoo
complete	confute	quatorze
complex	congeal	_____
comply	congest	_____
compose	conjoin	_____
composed	conjunct	_____
compress	connect	_____
compressed	connive	_____
comprise	connote	_____
compute	consent	_____
conceal	conserve	_____
concede	consign	_____

LA /lə/—two syllables

lacrosse	lapel	_____
lagoon	legit	_____
lament	_____	_____

MA /mə/—two syllables

macaque	masseur	_____
macaw	masseuse	_____
machine	mature	_____
massage	_____	_____

PA /pə/—two syllables

panache	petite	pollute
papoose	pizazz	possess
passade	police	puccoon
patrol	policed	_____
pelisse	polite	_____

RA /rə/—two syllables

ramose	ravine	_____
rapport	regime	_____
rattan	_____	_____

SA /sə/—two syllables

salaam	subserve	suggest
salon	subside	supplant
saloop	subsist	supplies
salute	subsume	supply
severe	subtend	support
subdue	subtract	suppose
subject	subvert	supposed
subjoin	succeed	suppress
sublime	success	supreme
submerge	succinct	suspect
submerse	succumb	suspend
submit	suffice	suspire
subscribe	suffuse	sustain

A

SHA /ʃə/ — two syllables

chagrin	chenille	shebang
chamade	shagreen	shellac
chemise	shallot	_____

TA /tə/ — two syllables

taboo	toward	_____
tonight	towards	_____

VA /və/ — two syllables

valise	velure	volute
velour	veneer	_____

YA /jə/ — two syllables

yapok	_____	_____

ZHA /ʒə/ — two syllables

jeté	_____	_____

A /ə/ — final

a	the	_____

E /i/

E /i/ — one syllable

each · eat · eke
ease · eaves · eve
east · eel · _____

E /i/ — two syllables

eager · eating · eon
eagle · eavesdrop · equal
eaglet · edict · equine
easeful · educt · ether
easel · ego · ethos
easement · egress · even
eastern · egret · evening
eastward · either · evil
easy · eland · _____
eater · emu · _____

BE /bi/ — one syllable

be · bean · beep
beach · beast · beet
bead · beat · _____
beak · bee · _____
beam · beef · _____

BE /bi/ — two syllables

beachfront · beading · beamy
beachhead · beadwork · beanbag
beachside · beady · beanie
beachwear · beagle · beanpole
beacon · beaker · beanstalk
beaded · beaming · beaten

E

beater	beehive	beyond
beaver	beeline	_____
bebop	beeper	_____
beechnut	beeswax	_____
beechwood	beetle	_____
beefsteak	being	_____

CHE /tʃi/ —one syllable

cheap	cheep	_____
cheat	cheese	_____
cheek	chief	_____

CHE /tʃi/ —two syllables

cheapen	cheesecloth	chieftain
cheater	cheetah	_____
cheekbone	chiefdom	_____
cheesecake	chiefly	_____

DE /di/ —one syllable

deal	deed	deep
dean	deem	_____

DE /di/ —two syllables

dealer	deep-fry	deplane
debrief	deeply	depot
decal	deep-sea	detour
decent	defect	detrain
decoy	defog	diesel
deepen	defuse	_____
deeper	defy	_____
deep-freeze	degrade	_____

FE /fi/ —one syllable

feast	feel	fiend
feat	feet	_____
fee	fief	_____
feed	field	_____

FE /fi/—two syllables

feaster	feedlot	fielder
feature	feeler	fieldwork
feeble	feeling	_____
feebly	feline	_____
feedback	female	_____
feeder	femur	_____
feeding	fever	_____

GE /gi/—one syllable

geese	ghee	_____

GE /gi/—two syllables

geezer	_____	_____

HE /hi/—one syllable

he	heave	he'll
heal	he'd	he's
heap	heed	_____
heat	heel	_____
heath	heeled	_____

HE /hi/—two syllables

healer	heatstroke	heehaw
healing	heave-ho	heeler
heaper	heaver	heelless
heated	heaving	helix
heater	heedful	_____
heathen	heedless	_____

JE /dʒi/—one syllable

gee	gene	jeans

JE /dʒi/—two syllables

genial	genome	geoid
genie	genus	jeepers
genius	geode	_____

E

KE /ki/—one syllable

keel	key	quay
keen	keyed	quiche
keep	keys	_____

KE /ki/—two syllables

keelage	keloid	kilo
keelboat	keno	kiosk
keener	ketone	kiva
keenly	keyboard	kiwi
keenness	keyhole	quayage
keeper	keynote	_____
keeping	keypad	_____
keepsake	keystroke	_____

LE /li/—one syllable

leach	lease	leek
lead	leash	lief
leaf	least	liege
league	leave	lien
leak	leaves	_____
lean	lee	_____
leap	leech	_____

LE /li/—two syllables

leachy	leaner	legal
leader	leaning	legion
leading	leanly	leisure
lead-off	lean-to	lemur
leafage	leaper	lesion
leafless	leapfrog	lever
leaflet	leaping	liter
leafy	leapyear	_____
leaguer	leasing	_____
leakage	leaving	_____
leakproof	leeward	_____
leaky	leeway	

ME /mi/—one syllable

me	meat	mien
meal	meek	_____
mean	meet	_____
means	mete	_____

ME /mi/—two syllables

meager	meantime	meeker
mealtime	meanwhile	meekly
mealy	measles	meeting
meaning	measly	megrim
meanly	meatball	meow
meanness	meatless	meter

NE /ni/—one syllable

knead	neap	needs
knee	neat	niece
kneel	need	_____

NE /ni/—two syllables

kneecap	neatness	needn't
knee-deep	neato	needy
kneepad	needful	neither
neater	needle	neon
neatly	needless	nevus

PE /pi/—one syllable

peace	peat	peep
peach	peek	peeve
peak	peel	piece
peal	peen	pique

PE /pi/—two syllables

peaceful	peahen	peeler
peachy	peaked	peeling
peacock	peanut	peeper
pea-green	peavey	peephole

E

peevish	people	pilaf
peewee	piecemeal	piquant
pekoe	piecework	piton
penal	piecing	pizza

RE /ri/ —one syllable

reach	reed	wreak
read	reef	wreath
real	reek	wreathe
ream	reel	_____
reap	reeve	_____

RE /ri/ —two syllables

reacher	recourse	rematch
react	redress	renal
reader	reeffish	repaint
reading	reeler	replay
real	refill	resale
reamer	reflex	research
reaper	refund	reset
reason	regain	reship
rebate	regal	resource
rebirth	regent	retail
rebound	region	retake
rebuff	regress	rethink
rebuke	regroup	retouch
rebus	rehash	retread
recall	reject	revamp
recap	rejoin	rewind
recent	rekey	rewire
recess	relapse	reword
recharge	relay	rework
recoil	release	rewrite

SE /si/ —one syllable

cease	seam	seen
cede	seat	seep
scene	see	seethe
sea	seed	seize
seal	seek	siege
seals	seem	_____

SE /si/ —two syllables

cease-fire	seaside	seeming
cedar	season	seemly
ceiling	seating	seepage
scenic	seatwork	seesaw
seaboard	seaward	seizer
seafood	seaway	seizure
sealant	seaweed	senile
sealer	secant	senior
seamster	secret	sequel
seamstress	seeder	sequence
seaplane	seedling	sequent
seaport	seedy	sequin
seashell	seeing	_____
seashore	seeker	_____
seasick	seemer	_____

SHE /ʃi/ —one syllable

chic	sheave	sheik
she	she'd	she'll
sheaf	sheen	she's
sheath	sheep	shield
sheathe	sheet	_____

SHE /ʃi/ —two syllables

chicly	sheeny	sheepish
chignon	sheep-dip	sheepskin
sheathing	sheepdog	sheeting
sheefish	sheepfold	shieldless

TE /ti/—one syllable

tea	tease	teethe
teach	tee	_____
teak	teen	_____
teal	teens	_____
team	teeth	_____

TE /ti/—two syllables

teacake	teamwork	teeny
teacart	teapot	teeter
teacher	teaser	teether
teaching	teashop	teething
teacup	teaspoon	tepee
teahouse	teatime	T-shirt
teakwood	teeming	_____
teammate	teenage	_____
teamster	teensy	_____

THE /ði/—one syllable

the	these	_____
thee	_____	_____

THE /θi/—one syllable

theme	thieve	_____
thief	_____	_____

THE /θi/—two syllables

theist	thesis	_____
thema	thievish	_____

VE /vi/—one syllable

veal	veep	_____
vee	_____	_____

VE /vi/—two syllables

V-eight	velum	venous
velar	venal	veto

E

WE /wi/—one syllable

we	weave	weep
weak	we'd	we'll
weal	wee	we've
weald	weed	wield
wean	week	_____

WE /wi/—two syllables

weaken	weaving	weeny
weaker	weeder	weeper
weakling	weedy	weeping
weakness	weekdays	weepy
weanling	weekend	weevil
weasel	weekly	wielder
weaver	weeknight	wieldy

WHE /ʍi/—one syllable

whee	wheeled	_____
wheel	wheeze	_____

WHE /ʍi/—two syllables

wheedle	wheelie	wheezy
wheelchair	wheeling	_____
wheeler	wheezer	_____

YE /ji/—one syllable

ye	yeast	yield

YE /ji/—two syllables

yeasty	yielding	_____

ZE /zi/—one syllable

zeal	_____	_____

ZE /zi/—two syllables

zebra	zenith	_____
zebu	zealless	_____

E /i/—final

be	lee	thee
bee	me	three
dee	plea	tree
fee	quay	vee
flea	scree	we
flee	sea	wee
free	see	whee
gee	she	ye
ghee	ski	_____
glee	spree	_____
he	tea	_____
key	tee	_____
knee	the	_____

EB /ib/—final

glebe	plebe	_____
grebe	_____	_____

ECH /itʃ/—final

beach	each	reach
beech	leach	screech
bleach	leech	speech
breach	peach	teach
breech	preach	_____

ED /id/—final

bead	heed	she'd
bleed	keyed	speed
breed	knead	steed
cede	lead	teed
creed	need	treed
deed	plead	tweed
feed	read	we'd
freed	reed	weed
greed	screed	_____
he'd	seed	_____

ELD /ild/—final

field	reeled	wield
heeled	shield	yield
keeled	squealed	_____
kneeled	steeled	_____
pealed	weald	_____
peeled	wheeled	_____

END /ind/—final

cleaned	leaned	screened
gleaned	preened	weaned

EF /if/—final

beef	grief	sheaf
brief	leaf	thief
chief	lief	_____
fief	reef	_____

EG /ig/—final

gigue	_____	_____
league	_____	_____

EJ /idʒ/—final

liege	_____	_____
siege	_____	_____

EK /ik/—final

beak	meek	squeak
bleak	peak	streak
cheek	peek	teak
chic	reek	tweak
clique	seek	weak
creak	sheik	week
creek	shriek	wreak
freak	sleek	_____
leak	sneak	_____
leek	speak	_____

EL /il/—final

creel	peal	teal
deal	peel	veal
eel	real	weal
feel	reel	we'll
heal	seal	wheel
heel	she'll	zeal
he'll	spiel	_____
keel	squeal	_____
kneel	steal	_____
meal	steel	_____

EM /im/—final

beam	scheme	team
cream	scream	theme
deem	seam	_____
dream	seem	_____
gleam	steam	_____
ream	stream	_____

EN /in/—final

bean	lean	sheen
clean	mean	spleen
dean	peen	teen
e'en	preen	'tween
gene	queen	wean
glean	scene	_____
green	screen	_____
keen	seen	_____

EP /ip/—final

beep	keep	sleep
bleep	leap	steep
cheap	neap	sweep
cheep	peep	veep
creep	reap	weep
deep	seep	_____
heap	sheep	_____

ES /is/ —final

cease	grease	piece
crease	lease	_____
fleece	niece	_____
geese	peace	_____

ESH /iʃ/ —final

leash	_____	_____
quiche	_____	_____

ET /it/ —final

beat	meat	sweet
beet	meet	treat
bleat	neat	tweet
cheat	peat	wheat
cleat	pleat	_____
eat	seat	_____
feat	sheet	_____
feet	skeet	_____
fleet	sleet	_____
greet	street	_____
heat	suite	_____

EST /ist/ —final

beast	fleeced	yeast
ceased	leased	_____
creased	least	_____
east	pieced	_____
feast	priest	_____

ETH /ið/ —final

breathe	teethe	_____
seethe	wreathe	_____

ETH /iθ/ —final

heath	teeth	_____
sheath	wreath	_____

EV /iv/—final

breve	heave	sleave
cleave	leave	sleeve
eve	peeve	thieve
greave	reeve	weave
grieve	sheave	we've

EZ /iz/—final

bees	keys	squeeze
breeze	knees	tease
cheese	peas	these
ease	please	threes
fees	seas	trees
fleas	seize	tweeze
freeze	she's	wheeze
frieze	skis	_____
he's	sneeze	_____

EVZ /ivz/—final

eaves	sheaves	thieves
leaves	sleeves	_____

EZH /iʒ/—final

liege	_____	_____

E /ɛ/

E /ɛ/ — one syllable

ebb	elk	elves
edge	ell	em
egg	elm	end
elf	else	etch

E /ɛ/ — two syllables

any	emcee	engross
echo	empire	engulf
eddy	employ	enhance
edger	empress	enjoy
edgeways	empty	enlarge
edging	enact	enlist
edgy	encamp	enmesh
edit	enchant	enrage
effort	enclave	enrich
eggnog	enclose	enroll
eggplant	encode	ensign
eggshell	endear	ensue
elbow	ending	ensure
elder	endive	entail
eldest	endless	enter
elfin	endorse	enthrall
elfish	endow	enthrone
embalm	endure	enthuse
embark	enface	entice
embed	enfold	entire
ember	enforce	entrance
emblem	engage	entrench
emboss	engine	entry
embrace	engrave	envoy

57

envy	ethnic	export
enzyme	ever	extant
epic	every	extra
epoch	exarch	X-ray
escort	excess	_____
essay	excise	_____
essence	exhale	_____
estate	exile	_____
esteem	exit	_____
etcher	expert	_____
etching	explant	_____
ethic	exploit	_____

BE /bɛ/ — one syllable

beck	belt	bet
bed	ben	_____
beg	bench	_____
belch	bend	_____
bell	bent	_____
belle	best	_____

BE /bɛ/ — two syllables

beckon	bedspread	bench-press
bedbug	bedtime	bentwood
bedding	beggar	better
bedlam	belfry	betting
bedlamp	bellhop	bevel
bedlight	bellow	beverage
bedpost	bellows	bevy
bedrock	belly	_____
bedroll	bencher	_____
bedroom	benchmark	_____

CHE /tʃɛ/ — one syllable

check	chest	_____
checks	_____	_____
chess	_____	_____

CHE /tʃɛ/ —two syllables

cellist	checkmate	chessboard
cello	checkoff	chestnut
checkbook	check-out	_____
checker	checkpoint	_____
checkered	checkup	_____
checking	cheddar	_____

DE /dɛ/ —one syllable

dead	deck	dent
deaf	deft	desk
death	dell	_____
debt	den	_____

DE /dɛ/ —two syllables

deadbeat	deafen	denim
deadbolt	deafer	dental
deaden	deathly	dentist
dead-end	debit	denture
deadeye	debtless	desert
deadline	debtor	desktop
deadlock	decade	_____
deadly	decking	_____
deadwood	deckle	_____

FE /fɛ/ —one syllable

fed	fen	fetch
fell	fence	fez
felt	fend	_____

FE /fɛ/ —two syllables

feather	fencing	fetid
feldspar	fender	fetish
fellow	fennel	fetlock
felon	festive	fettle
felting	festoon	_____
fencer	fetcher	_____

GE /gɛ/ —one syllable

get	guess	guest

GE /gɛ/ —two syllables

gelding	ghetto	guesswork
get-up	guesser	guesthouse

HE /hɛ/ —one syllable

head	held	hence
health	helm	_____
heck	hem	_____
hedge	hemp	_____
heft	hen	_____

HE /hɛ/ —two syllables

headache	headstone	hello
headband	headstrong	helmet
headboard	headway	helper
headed	headwork	helpful
header	healthful	helping
headfirst	healthy	helpless
headgear	heather	helpmate
heading	heaven	hemline
headlamp	heavy	hemlock
headland	heckle	hemmer
headlight	hectare	hemming
headline	hectic	hemstitch
headlong	hedgehog	henceforth
headphone	hedger	henna
headpiece	hedgerow	heptad
headrest	hedgy	hessite
headset	hefty	_____
headstand	heifer	_____

JE /dʒɛ/ —one syllable

gel	gent	jest
gem	jell	jet

JE /dʒɛ/ —two syllables

gelid	gentry	jester
gender	gesture	jetport
genteel	jealous	jetsam
gentile	jelly	jetty
gentle	jestbook	_____

KE /kɛ/ —one syllable

kedge	kempt	ketch
kelp	ken	_____
kemp	kept	_____

KE /kɛ/ —two syllables

chemist	kestrel	kettle
kennel	ketchup	kevel

LE /lɛ/ —one syllable

lead	left	lent
leant	leg	less
leapt	lend	lest
led	length	let
ledge	lens	_____

LE /lɛ/ —two syllables

leaden	legume	lesson
leading	lemming	lessor
leather	lemon	letdown
leaven	lender	letter
lectern	lending	letting
lection	lengthen	lettuce
lector	lengthwise	letup
lecture	lengthy	levee
ledger	lentil	level
left-hand	leopard	lever
legate	lessee	levy
legend	lessen	_____
leggings	lesser	_____

ME /mɛ/—one syllable

meant	men	mess
meld	mend	met
melt	mesh	_____

ME /mɛ/—two syllables

meadow	member	mesquite
measure	memo	message
measured	memoir	messroom
medal	menace	messy
meddle	mender	metal
medic	mending	methane
medley	mental	method
mellow	menthol	metric
melon	mention	mettle
meltdown	mentor	_____
melter	menu	_____
melting	meshwork	_____

NE /nɛ/—one syllable

knell	neck	next
knelt	nest	_____
neb	net	_____

NE /nɛ/—two syllables

necklace	nether	nexus
necktie	netting	_____
nectar	nettle	_____
nephew	network	_____
nestle	never	_____
nestling	next-door	_____

PE /pɛ/—one syllable

peck	pen	pep
peg	pence	pest
pelf	pend	pet
pelt	pent	_____

PE /pɛ/—two syllables

peasant	penance	pepper
pebble	pencil	peppy
pebbly	pendant	peptalk
pectin	pending	peptic
pedal	penguin	pesky
pedant	penknife	pestle
peddle	pennant	petal
peddler	penny	petty
pegboard	penpoint	_____
pegging	pension	_____
pellet	pensive	_____
pelvis	penthouse	_____

RE /rɛ/—one syllable

read	rep	wren
realm	rest	wrench
red	retch	wrest
ref	rev	_____
rend	rex	_____
rent	wreck	_____

RE /rɛ/—two syllables

ready	redwood	restful
rebel	refuge	resting
reckless	refuse	restive
reckon	regnant	restless
recluse	relic	revel
record	relish	wreckage
redbird	remnant	wrecker
redbud	render	wrestle
redcap	rental	wrestler
redden	renter	_____
redder	reptile	_____
reddish	rescue	_____
redhead	resin	_____
redness	respite	_____

SE /sɛ/—one syllable

cell	sect	sent
cense	sedge	set
cent	self	sex
said	sell	_____
says	send	_____
scent	sense	_____

SE /sɛ/—two syllables

cellar	self-love	septum
censor	self-serve	session
censure	self-talk	setback
census	self-taught	setoff
centaur	self-worth	settee
center	seller	setter
centered	selling	setting
central	sellout	settle
second	seltzer	settler
section	semblance	seven
sector	senate	seventh
segment	sender	sever
seldom	send-off	sextant
self-care	sensate	sextet
self-help	senseless	sexton
selfhood	sentence	_____
selfish	sentry	_____
selfless	septic	_____

SHE /ʃɛ/—one syllable

chef	shelf	shelve
shed	shell	_____

SHE /ʃɛ/—two syllables

chevron	shellproof	shelving
shedding	shellwork	shepherd
shekel	shelter	_____
shellfish	shelty	_____

E

TE /tɛ/—one syllable

tell	tense	text
tempt	tent	_____
ten	tenth	_____
tend	test	_____

TE /tɛ/—two syllables

technique	tender	tenure
teddy	tendon	tepid
telex	tendril	testate
teller	tenet	test-drive
telling	tenfold	testee
telltale	tennis	tester
temper	tenor	testy
tempered	tensely	tether
tempest	tenseness	textbook
template	tensile	textile
temple	tension	texture
tempo	ten-speed	_____
tenant	tented	_____

THE /ðɛ/—one syllable

them	_____	_____
then	_____	_____
thence	_____	_____

THE /ðɛ/—two syllables

themselves	_____	_____
thenceforth	_____	_____

THE /θɛ/—one syllable

theft	_____	_____

VE /vɛ/—one syllable

veld	vest	vex
vend	vet	vexed
vent	vetch	_____

VE /vɛ/—two syllables

vector	ventral	vested
vellum	venture	vestige
velvet	venue	vestment
vendor	vesper	vestry
venom	vessel	_____

WE /wɛ/—one syllable

wealth	weft	wend
web	weld	went
webbed	well	wept
wed	welsh	west
wedge	welt	wet

WE /wɛ/—two syllables

wealthy	welder	well-worn
weapon	welfare	welter
weather	well-done	westbound
weathered	well-fixed	western
webbing	well-known	westward
webfeet	well-made	wetland
webfoot	wellness	wetness
wedded	well-off	_____
wedding	well-read	_____
wedlock	wellspring	_____
welcome	well-timed	_____

WHE /ʍɛ/—one syllable

whelk	whelp	whence
whelm	when	whet

WHE /ʍɛ/—two syllables

whether	whetstone	whetter

YE /jɛ/—one syllable

yell	yen	yet
yelp	yes	_____

E

YE /jɛ/ —two syllables

yellow	yelper	_____

ZE /zɛ/ —one syllable

zed	zest	_____

ZE /zɛ/ —two syllables

zealot	zephyr	_____
zealous	zestful	_____

EB /ɛb/ —final

ebb	neb	web

ECH /ɛtʃ/ —final

etch	retch	vetch
fetch	sketch	_____
ketch	stretch	_____

ELCH /ɛltʃ/ —final

belch	welch	_____
squelch	_____	_____

ENCH /ɛntʃ/ —final

bench	quench	wrench
blench	stench	_____
clench	tench	_____
drench	trench	_____

ED /ɛd/ —final

bed	lead	sled
bled	led	sped
bread	pled	spread
dead	read	stead
dread	red	thread
fed	said	tread
fled	shed	wed
head	shred	zed

ELD /ɛld/—final

geld	quelled	swelled
held	shelled	weld
jelled	smelled	yelled
meld	spelled	_____

END /ɛnd/—final

bend	mend	trend
blend	penned	vend
end	rend	wend
fend	send	yenned
friend	spend	_____
lend	tend	

EF /ɛf/—final

chef	deaf	_____
clef	ref	_____

ELF /ɛlf/—final

elf	self	_____
pelf	shelf	_____

EG /ɛg/—final

beg	egg	peg
dreg	leg	skeg

EJ /ɛdʒ/—final

dredge	ledge	wedge
edge	pledge	_____
fledge	sedge	_____
hedge	sledge	_____

EK /ɛk/—final

beck	heck	trek
check	neck	wreck
deck	peck	_____
fleck	speck	_____

ELK /ɛlk/ —final
elk _____ _____
whelk _____ _____

ESK /ɛsk/ —final
desk _____ _____

E

EL /ɛl/ —final

bell	knell	swell
belle	quell	tell
cell	sell	well
dell	shell	yell
dwell	smell	_____
fell	snell	_____
gel	spell	_____
jell	steppe	_____

EM /ɛm/ —final

em	phlegm	them
gem	rem	_____
hem	stem	_____

ELM /ɛlm/ —final

elm	realm	_____
helm	whelm	_____

EN /ɛn/ —final

ben	ken	when
den	men	wren
fen	pen	yen
glen	ten	_____
hen	then	_____
		_____

EP /ɛp/ —final

pep	skep	_____
prep	step	_____
rep	strep	_____

ELP /ɛlp/—final

help	skelp	yelp
kelp	whelp	_____

EMP /ɛmp/—final

hemp	kemp	_____

ES /ɛs/—final

bless	fess	press
chess	guess	stress
cress	less	tress
dress	mess	yes

EKS /ɛks/—final

checks	flex	specs
decks	rex	treks
flecks	sex	vex

ENS /ɛns/—final

cense	hence	tense
dense	pence	thence
fence	sense	whence

ESH /ɛʃ/—final

flesh	mesh	_____
fresh	thresh	_____

ET /ɛt/—final

bet	met	threat
debt	net	vet
fret	pet	wet
get	set	yet
jet	stet	_____
let	sweat	_____

EFT /ɛft/—final

cleft	heft	theft
deft	left	weft

E

ELT /εlt/—final

belt	melt	welt
dealt	pelt	_____
dwelt	smelt	_____
felt	spelt	_____
knelt	veldt	_____

EMPT /εmpt/—final

dreamt	kempt	tempt

ENT /εnt/—final

bent	meant	spent
cent	pent	tent
dent	rent	vent
gent	scent	went
lent	sent	_____

EPT /εpt/—final

crept	prepped	swept
kept	slept	wept
pepped	stepped	_____

EST /εst/—final

best	lest	stressed
blessed	messed	test
chest	nest	vest
crest	pest	west
dressed	pressed	wrest
guest	quest	zest
jest	rest	_____

EKST /εkst/—final

flexed	text	_____
next	vexed	_____

ETH /εθ/—final

breath	death	_____

EDTH /ɛdθ/—final
breadth   _____   _____

ELTH /ɛlθ/—final
health   wealth   _____
stealth   _____   _____

ENGTH /ɛŋθ/—final
length   strength   _____

EV /ɛv/—final
breve   _____   _____
rev   _____   _____

ELV /ɛlv/—final
delve   _____   _____
shelve   _____   _____
twelve   _____   _____

EGZ /ɛgz/—final
begs   dregs   pegs
eggs   legs   _____

I /aɪ/

I /aɪ/ — one syllable

aisle

aye

eye

I

ice

iced

I'd

I'll

I'm

isle

I've

_____

_____

_____

_____

I /aɪ/ — two syllables

eider

either

eyeball

eyebrow

eyecup

eyedrop

eyeful

eyeglass

eyelash

eyelet

eyelid

eyesight

eyesore

eyestrain

eyetooth

eyewash

eyewear

eyewink

iamb

ibex

ibis

iceberg

iceboat

icebound

icebox

icecap

ice-cold

icefall

icehouse

icequake

ice-skate

icing

icon

icy

idle

idol

ion

iron

island

islet

item

ivy

ylem

_____

_____

_____

_____

BI /baɪ/ — one syllable

bide

bight

bike

bile

bind

bine

bite

buy

by

bye

byte

_____

_____

_____

_____

BI /baɪ/—two syllables

bias	biplane	bygone
biceps	bisect	bylaw
bifid	bison	byline
biker	biting	bypass
binder	bivalve	by-path
binding	buyer	byway
biped	bye-bye	_____

CIII /tʃaɪ/—one syllable

chide	chime	chive
child	chine	

CHI /tʃaɪ/—two syllables

chider	childish	_____
chiding	childlike	_____
childhood	chiming	_____

DI /daɪ/—one syllable

dial	dike	dive
dice	dime	dye
die	dine	dyne

DI /daɪ/—two syllables

dial	digress	diverge
diamond	dilate	diverse
diaper	dilute	divert
dicey	diner	divest
die-hard	dinette	diving
diet	dining	dyad
digest	diode	_____
digraph	diver	_____

FI /faɪ/—one syllable

fie	file	five
fife	find	_____
fight	fine	_____

FI /faɪ/ —two syllables

fiber	filing	finer
fibroid	final	finespun
fighter	finals	finite
fighting	finance	fivefold
filar	finder	phylum
filer	finding	_____

GI /gaɪ/ —one syllable

guide	guise	_____
guile	guy	_____

GI /gaɪ/ —two syllables

geyser	guidepost	guileless
guidance	guider	_____
guidebook	guiding	_____
guideline	guileful	_____

HI /haɪ/ —one syllable

height	hie	hind
hi	high	hive
hide	hike	_____

HI /haɪ/ —two syllables

heighten	highland	hiker
hiding	highlight	hindmost
highboy	highly	hindsight
highbrow	highness	hydrant
highchair	high-priced	hydrous
high-class	high-rise	hygiene
higher	highroad	hyper
highest	high-toned	hyphen
high-grade	highway	_____
high-hat	hijack	_____

JI /dʒaɪ/ —one syllable

jibe	jive

JI /dʒaɪ/—two syllables

giant	jiver	jiving

KI /kaɪ/—one syllable

kind	kine	kite

KI /kaɪ/—two syllables

cayenne	kinder	kindness
cayuse	kindest	kiter
coyotc	kindly	_____

LI /laɪ/—one syllable

lice	like	lithe
lie	lime	live
life	line	lye
light	lined	_____

LI /laɪ/—two syllables

liar	lighten	lilac
libel	lighthouse	limeade
license	lighting	limekiln
lichen	lightly	limelight
lifeboat	lightness	limestone
lifeful	lightning	liner
lifeguard	lightship	lineup
lifelike	lightweight	lining
life-size	light-year	lion
lifestyle	likely	lithely
lifetime	likeness	lively
lifework	likewise	lying
lightboat	liking	_____

MI /maɪ/—one syllable

mice	mile	mise
might	mime	mite
mike	mind	my
mild	mine	_____

MI /maɪ/—two syllables

mica	mileage	minus
micro	milepost	minute
microbe	miler	miser
micron	milestone	miter
mighty	milo	myna
migraine	minded	myself
migrant	minder	_____
migrate	mindful	_____
milder	mind-set	_____
mildest	miner	_____
mildly	mining	_____
mildness	minor	

NI /naɪ/—one syllable

knife	nigh	_____
knight	night	_____
knives	nine	_____
nice	ninth	_____
_____		_____

NI /naɪ/—two syllables

knighthood	night-light	nitrate
nicely	nightly	nitric
nicer	nightmare	nitrite
nidus	nightstand	nitrous
nightfall	nighttime	nylon
nightgown	nightwear	_____
nighthawk	nineteen	_____
nightie	nineteenth	_____
nightlife	ninety	_____

PI /paɪ/—one syllable

pi	pile	piped
pie	pine	_____
pied	pint	_____
pike	pipe	_____

PI /paɪ/—two syllables

pica	piling	piper
piebald	pilot	pipette
piecrust	pinesap	piping
pika	piney	pylon
pilar	pious	python
pileup	pipeline	_____

RI /raɪ/—one syllable

rhyme	rile	rive
rice	rime	rye
ride	rind	wright
rife	ripe	write
right	rise	writhe
rights	rite	wry

RI /raɪ/—two syllables

rhinestone	rightful	rival
rhino	right-hand	write-in
rhymer	rightly	write-off
rhymester	right-on	writer
rider	riot	write-up
riding	ripen	writing
rifeness	ripeness	wryly
righteous	riser	wryness
righter	rising	_____

SI /saɪ/—one syllable

cite	sigh	sine
psych	sight	site
side	sign	size

SI /saɪ/—two syllables

cider	cycling	cypress
cipher	cyclist	psychic
cycle	cycloid	sideboard
cyclic	cyclone	sideburns

sidecar	sidle	silence
sided	sighing	silent
sidekick	sighted	silo
sideline	sightless	sinus
sideshow	sightly	siphon
sideswipe	sight-read	sisal
sidetrack	sightsee	sizing
sidewalk	signboard	_____
sidewall	signer	_____
sideward	sign-off	_____
sideways	signpost	_____
siding	silage	_____

SHI /ʃaɪ/—one syllable

shied	shine	shy

SHI /ʃaɪ/—two syllables

shier	shining	_____
shiner	shiny	_____

TI /taɪ/—one syllable

thyme	tights	tine
tide	tile	tithe
tie	tiled	tyke
tight	time	type
	times	

TI /taɪ/—two syllables

tidal	tiger	timely
tideland	tighten	time-out
tidemark	tightrope	timer
tideway	tightwad	timework
tidings	tigress	timing
tidy	tiler	tiny
tie-dye	tiling	titan
tie-in	timecard	tithing
tier	time-lag	title
tie-up	timeless	titrate

tycoon	typhoon	typo
typeface	typhus	_____
typeset	typing	_____
typhoid	typist	_____

THI /ðaɪ/—one syllable

thine	thy	_____

THI /ðaɪ/—two syllables

thyself	_____	_____

THI /θaɪ/—one syllable

thigh	_____	_____

THI /θaɪ/—two syllables

thighbone	thymus	_____

VI /vaɪ/—one syllable

vibes	vine	_____
vice	vined	_____
vie	vise	_____
vile	_____	_____

VI /vaɪ/—two syllables

via	vileness	visor
vial	vineland	vital
viand	viny	_____
vibrant	vinyl	_____
vibrate	viol	_____
viceroy	viper	_____

WI /waɪ/—one syllable

wide	wipe	_____
wife	wise	_____
wild	withe	_____
wile	wive	_____
wind	wives	_____

WI /waɪ/—two syllables

widen	wilder	winding
wider	wildfire	wipeout
widespread	wildfowl	wiper
widest	wildlife	wisecrack
wifely	wily	wiser
wildcat	winder	wisest

WHI /ʍaɪ/—one syllable

while	white	_____
whilst	why	_____
whine		_____

WHI /ʍaɪ/—two syllables

whiner	whitefish	whiter
whiny	whiten	whitest
whitecap	whiteness	whitewash
white-faced	whiteout	whitish

YI /jaɪ/—one syllable

yipe	yite	_____

ZI /zaɪ/—one syllable

zyme	_____	_____

ZI /zaɪ/—two syllables

xylan	xyloid	zymase
xylem	xylose	_____
xylene	zygote	_____

I /aɪ/—final

aye	dry	guy
buy	dye	hi
by	eye	high
bye	fie	lie
cry	fly	lye
die	fry	my

nigh	sky	try
pi	sly	vie
pie	spry	why
ply	spy	wry
pry	sty	_____
rye	thigh	_____
shy	thy	_____
sigh	tie	_____

IB /aɪb/—final

bribe	scribe	vibe
jibe	tribe	_____

ID /aɪd/—final

bide	I'd	spied
bride	lied	stride
chide	pied	tide
cried	plied	tied
died	pride	tried
dried	pried	vied
dyed	ride	wide
fried	shied	_____
glide	side	_____
guide	slide	_____
hide	snide	_____

ILD /aɪld/—final

child	piled	tiled
dialed	riled	wild
filed	smiled	_____
mild	styled	_____

IMD /aɪmd/—final

chimed	primed	_____
climbed	rhymed	_____
grimed	slimed	_____
mimed	timed	_____

IND /aɪnd/—final

bind	lined	tined
blind	mind	twined
dined	mined	vined
find	pined	whined
fined	rind	wind
grind	shined	_____
hind	signed	_____
kind	spined	_____

IF /aɪf/—final

fife	life	strife
knife	rife	wife

IK /aɪk/—final

bike	pike	tyke
dike	psych	_____
hike	spike	_____
like	strike	_____
mike	trike	_____

IL /aɪl/—final

aisle	pile	vile
bile	rile	while
dial	smile	wile
file	stile	_____
guile	style	_____
I'll	tile	_____
mile	trial	_____

IM /aɪm/—final

chime	mime	time
climb	prime	zyme
dime	rhyme	_____
grime	rime	_____
I'm	slime	_____
lime	thyme	_____

IN /aɪn/—final

bine	pine	tine
brine	shine	twine
dine	shrine	vine
fine	sign	whine
kine	sine	_____
line	spine	_____
mine	swine	_____
nine	thine	_____

IP /aɪp/—final

gripe	stripe	wipe
pipe	swipe	yipe
ripe	tripe	_____
snipe	type	_____

IS /aɪs/—final

dice	rice	twice
ice	slice	vice
lice	spice	vise
mice	splice	_____
nice	thrice	_____
price	trice	_____

IKS /aɪks/—final

bikes	mikes	trikes
dikes	pikes	tykes
hikes	spikes	yikes
likes	strikes	_____

IT /aɪt/—final

bite	flight	might
blight	fright	mite
bright	height	night
byte	kite	plight
cite	knight	quite
fight	light	right

rite	sprite	_____
sight	tight	_____
site	trite	_____
slight	white	_____
smite	wright	_____
spite	write	_____

INT /aɪnt/ —final
pint	_____	_____

IPT /aɪpt/ —final
griped	swiped	_____
piped	typed	_____
sniped	wiped	_____
striped	_____	_____

IST /aɪst/ —final
diced	sliced	_____
iced	spiced	_____
priced	spliced	_____
riced	vised	_____

ITH /aɪð/ —final
blithe	tithe	_____
lithe	writhe	_____
scythe	_____	_____

INTH /aɪnθ/ —final
ninth	_____	_____

IV /aɪv/ —final
chive	jive	wive
dive	live	_____
drive	rive	_____
five	shrive	_____
hive	strive	_____
I've	thrive	_____

IZ /aɪz/ —final

buys	lies	sties
cries	mise	thighs
dies	pies	ties
dries	prize	tries
dyes	rise	vies
eyes	shies	wise
flies	size	_____
fries	skies	_____
guys	spies	_____

I /ɪ/

I

I /ɪ/ — one syllable

if	inch	it
ill	ink	itch
imp	inn	its
in	is	

I /ɪ/ — two syllables

eclipse	evert	expense
efface	evict	expire
effect	evoke	export
effuse	evolve	expose
eject	exact	expound
elapse	exalt	exult
elate	exam	igloo
elect	exceed	illness
elite	excel	image
ellipse	except	impact
elope	excess	impair
elude	exchange	impart
emerge	excise	impasse
emit	excite	impeach
emote	exclude	impinge
enough	excuse	impish
equate	exempt	import
equip	exert	impose
escape	exhaust	impound
estate	exist	impulse
esteem	expand	impure
estray	expect	impute
evade	expel	inboard
event	expend	inborn

87

inbounds	inner	intern
incense	inning	into
inchworm	input	invert
incur	insect	invest
indeed	insert	invite
index	inset	invoice
inert	inside	invoke
infant	insight	involve
infer	insist	inward
infield	inspire	isn't
injure	insure	itching
inkling	insured	itchy
inky	intact	itself
inlaid	intend	_____
inland	intense	_____
in-law	intent	_____
inlet	inter	_____

BI /bɪ/—one syllable

been	bilge	bisque
bib	bilk	bit
bid	bill	build
big	bin	built

BI /bɪ/—two syllables

becalm	begrudge	bemire
because	beguile	bemoan
become	behalf	bemuse
bedeck	behave	beneath
befall	behind	benign
befell	behold	bequeath
befit	behoove	bequest
befog	belay	beseech
before	belief	beset
befriend	believe	beside
begin	belong	besides
begone	below	besiege

bestow	bigot	bishop
betray	bigwig	bitten
between	billboard	bitter
beyond	billet	bizarre
bicker	billfold	builder
bidden	billiard	building
bidder	billing	buildup
bidding	billion	built-in
bigger	billow	built-up
biggest	bingo	business
bighorn	biscuit	busy

CHI /tʃɪ/ —one syllable

chick	chin	chintz
chill	chinch	chip
chimp	chink	chit

CHI /tʃɪ/ —two syllables

chicken	chilly	chipmunk
chickpea	chimney	chipper
chigger	chinchy	chisel
chili	chipboard	chitchat

DI /dɪ/ —one syllable

did	din	dish
dig	ding	disk
dill	dint	ditch
dim	dip	_____

DI /dɪ/ —two syllables

debar	deceit	decree
debark	deceive	deduce
debase	decide	deduct
debate	declaim	deface
decal	declare	defame
decant	decline	default
decay	decrease	defeat

defect	deserve	dinghy
defend	design	dingo
defense	designed	dingy
defer	desire	dinky
define	dessert	dinner
deflate	destroy	diphthong
deflect	destruct	dipper
deform	detach	dipstick
defraud	detail	disband
defray	detain	disbar
defrost	detect	disburse
defunct	deter	discard
defy	detest	discern
degrade	detour	discharge
degree	detract	disclaim
deject	device	disclose
delay	devise	discord
delete	devoid	discount
delight	devote	discourse
delude	devour	discreet
demand	devout	discus
demean	dicker	discuss
demise	dictate	disdain
demur	diction	disease
depart	diddle	disgrace
depend	didn't	disguise
depict	differ	disgust
deplore	diffuse	dishcloth
deploy	digest	dishful
deport	digger	dishpan
depose	digit	dishrag
depress	digress	dishware
deprive	dilute	disjoin
descend	dimly	disjoint
descent	dimmer	diskette
describe	dimness	dislike
desert	dimple	dislodge

dismal	dissect	ditty
dismay	dissent	diverge
dismiss	dissolve	diverse
dismount	distal	divert
disown	distance	divest
dispatch	distant	divide
dispel	distaste	divine
dispense	distend	divorce
disperse	distinct	divulge
displace	distort	divvy
display	distract	dizzy
displease	distress	_____
dispose	district	_____
disproof	disturb	_____
disprove	disuse	_____
dispute	dither	_____
disrupt	ditto	_____

FI /fɪ/ —one syllable

fib	film	fist
fifth	filth	fit
fig	fin	fizz
filch	finch	_____
fill	fish	_____

FI /fɪ/ —two syllables

fickle	filet	finesse
fiction	filler	finger
fiddle	fill-in	finish
fiddler	filling	fishbowl
fidget	fill-up	fisher
fifteen	filly	fishhook
fifteenth	filming	fishing
fifty	filmy	fishnet
figment	filter	fishpond
figure	filthy	fishtail
filbert	finance	fishy

fission	fitting	fizzy
fissure	fixate	physics
fitful	fixing	physique
fitly	fixture	_____
fitness	fizzle	_____

GI /gɪ/ —one syllable

gib	gild	give
gift	gill	guild
gig	gilt	guilt

GI /gɪ/ —two syllables

gibbon	gingham	guilder
giddy	gismo	guildship
gifted	given	guiltless
gift-wrap	giver	guilty
giggle	giving	guitar
gimmick	gizzard	_____

HI /hɪ/ —one syllable

hick	hinge	hit
hid	hint	hitch
hill	hip	hymn
hilt	his	_____
him	hiss	_____

HI /hɪ/ —two syllables

hiccup	hilly	hippo
hidden	himself	hitchhike
hillock	hinder	hither
hillside	hipbone	hitter
hilltop	hippie	hymnal

JI /dʒɪ/ —one syllable

gist	jib	jilt
gym	jiff	jinx
gyp	jig	_____

JI /dʒɪ/ —two syllables

gibber	jiffy	jitney
giblet	jigger	jitter
gimcrack	jiggle	_____
ginger	jiggly	_____
gymnast	jigsaw	_____
gymsuit	jillion	_____
gypsum	jimmy	_____
gypsy	jingle	

KI /kɪ/ —one syllable

kick	kin	kit
kid	king	kith
kill	kink	_____
kiln	kip	_____
kilt	kiss	_____

KI /kɪ/ —two syllables

kibbutz	kidskin	kingship
kickback	killdeer	king-size
kickball	kilter	kinship
kickboard	kindle	kipper
kicker	kindling	kitchen
kickoff	kindred	kitten
kickstand	kinfolk	kitty
kickup	kingbird	_____
kidding	kingdom	_____
kidney	kingly	_____

LI /lɪ/ —one syllable

lick	link	lymph
lid	lint	lynx
lift	lip	_____
lilt	lisp	_____
limb	list	_____
limp	lit	_____
ling	live	_____

LI /lɪ/—two syllables

lifter	lingo	listing
lily	lingual	listless
limber	linguist	litmus
limbo	linkage	litter
limit	linseed	little
limo	lintel	liver
limpet	linty	livid
limpid	lipid	living
limply	lip-read	lizard
limpness	lipstick	_____
linden	liquid	_____
linen	lissome	_____
linger	listen	_____

MI /mɪ/—one syllable

mid	mill	mist
midst	mince	mitt
miff	mink	mix
mil	mint	myth
milk	miss	_____

MI /mɪ/—two syllables

midair	midterm	mincing
midcourse	midway	mingle
midday	midwife	mini
midden	miffy	minnow
middle	mildew	minstrel
midget	milieu	minute
midland	milkweed	mischief
midlife	milky	miscue
midline	miller	misfit
midnight	millet	mishap
midpoint	million	mishmash
midriff	millwork	misjudge
midship	mimic	mislay
midstream	mincemeat	mislead

mismatch	missive	mixture
misplace	misspell	mix-up
misplay	mistake	mystic
misprint	mister	mystique
misquote	misty	mythic
missile	misuse	_____
missing	mitten	_____
mission	mixer	_____

NI /nɪ/ — one syllable

knit	nick	nit
nib	nil	nix
niche	nip	nymph

NI /nɪ/ — two syllables

knickers	nibble	nimble
knickknack	nickel	nimbus
knitter	nicker	ninja
knitting	nickname	nipple
negate	nifty	nippy
neglect	niggle	nitpick

PI /pɪ/ — one syllable

pick	pinch	pit
pig	ping	pitch
pill	pink	pith
pin	pip	_____

PI /pɪ/ — two syllables

pickaxe	picture	pigment
picker	piddle	pigpen
picket	piddling	pigskin
picking	pidgin	pigtail
pickle	piffle	pilaf
pickup	pigeon	pilgrim
picky	piggy	pillar
picnic	piglet	pillbox

pillow	pinkish	pitchfork
pimple	pinpoint	pitfall
pinball	pinprick	pithy
pincers	pinstripe	pittance
pinch-hit	pinto	pitter
pinhole	pinwheel	pity
pinion	pinwork	pivot
pinkeye	piston	pixie
pinkie	pitcher	

RI /rɪ/—one syllable

rib	rig	rinse
rich	rill	rip
rick	rim	risk
rid	rimmed	wring
riff	ring	wrist
rift	rink	

RI /rɪ/—two syllables

rebel	redress	relax
rebuff	reduce	relay
rebuke	refer	release
rebut	refine	relent
recall	reflect	relief
recede	reform	relieve
receipt	refrain	rely
receive	refresh	remain
recess	refuse	remark
recite	refute	remind
reclaim	regard	remiss
recline	regress	remit
recoil	regret	remorse
record	rehearse	remote
recount	reject	remove
recruit	rejoice	renew
recur	relapse	renounce
redeem	relate	repair

repay
repeal
repeat
repel
repent
replace
reply
report
repose
repress
reprieve
reproach
repute
request
require
rescind
research
resent
reserve
reside
resign
resist
resolve
resort
resound
respect
response

restore
restrain
restrict
result
resume
retain
retire
retort
retrace
retract
retreat
retrieve
return
reveal
revenge
revere
reverse
revert
review
revise
revive
revoke
revolt
revolve
reward
rhythm
ribbon

richer
riches
rickshaw
riddance
riddle
rigid
rigor
ringer
ripcord
ripple
river
rivet
wriggle
wringer
wrinkle
wrinkly
wristband
wristlet
wristlock
written
_____
_____
_____
_____
_____
_____
_____

SI /sɪ/—one syllable

cinch
cyst
sib
sick
sieve
sift
silk
sill

silt
sin
since
sing
singe
sink
sip
sis

sit
six
sixth
sylph
sync
_____
_____
_____

SI /sɪ/—two syllables

cinder	sickle	single
cistern	sickly	singly
citric	sickness	sinkage
citron	sickroom	sinker
citrus	sifter	sinkhole
city	signal	sinless
civet	signet	sipid
civic	silken	sissy
civil	silkscreen	sister
cygnet	silkweed	sitter
cymbal	silkworm	sitting
cynic	silky	sit-up
cystic	silly	sixteen
scissors	silty	sixty
secede	silver	sizzle
seclude	simmer	symbol
secrete	simper	symptom
secure	simple	synapse
sedan	simplex	syndrome
sedate	simply	synod
select	sincere	syntax
sibling	sinew	system
sickbed	sinful	_____
sicker	singer	_____
sickish	singing	_____

SHI /ʃɪ/—one syllable

schist	shim	_____
shift	shin	_____
shill	ship	_____

SHI /ʃɪ/—two syllables

chiffon	shimmer	shingle
shiftless	shimmy	shinny
shifty	shinbone	shipboard
shilling	shindig	shipload

shipmate	shipside	_____
shipment	shipway	_____
shipper	shipwreck	_____
shipping	shipyard	_____
shipshape	shiver	_____

TI /tɪ/ —one syllable

tic	tilth	tip
tick	tin	_____
tiff	ting	_____
till	tinge	_____
tilt	tint	_____

TI /tɪ/ —two syllables

ticker	tinder	tippy
ticket	tinfoil	tiptoe
ticking	tingle	tiptop
tickle	tingly	tissue
ticklish	tinker	titmouse
ticktock	tinkly	titter
tidbit	tinny	tizzy
tilde	tinsel	_____
tillage	tinsmith	_____
tiller	tinter	_____
timbal	tinwork	_____
timber	tip-off	_____
timbrel	tipper	_____
timid	tippet	_____
tincture	tipping	_____

THI /ðɪ/ —one syllable

this	_____	_____

THI /θɪ/ —one syllable

thick	think	_____
thin	thinned	_____
thing	_____	

THI /θɪ/—two syllables

thicken	thinker	thin-skinned
thicket	thinking	thistle
thickish	thinly	thistly
thickness	thinner	thither
thick-skinned	thinness	_____
thimble	thinnish	

VI /vɪ/—one syllable

vim	_____	_____

VI /vɪ/—two syllables

vicar	villain	vision
victor	vineyard	visit
vigil	vintage	vista
vigor	visage	vivid
villa	viscose	_____
village	viscous	_____

WI /wɪ/—one syllable

wick	win	wish
width	wince	wisp
wig	winch	wit
will	wind	witch
willed	wing	with
wilt	wink	_____

WI /wɪ/—two syllables

wicked	willful	wind-borne
wicker	willies	windbreak
wicket	willing	windburn
widget	willow	winded
widow	wimble	windfall
widthwise	wimple	windlass
wiggle	windage	windmill
wigwag	wind-bell	window
wigwam	windblown	windpipe

windproof	winnow	withheld
windshield	winsome	withhold
windsock	winter	within
windstorm	wintry	without
windsurf	wisdom	withstand
wind-swept	wishbone	witness
windtight	wishful	witty
windward	wispy	wizard
windy	wistful	women
wingspan	withal	_____
wingspread	withdraw	_____
winker	withdrawn	_____
winkle	withdrew	_____
winner	wither	_____
winning	withers	_____

WHI /ʍɪ/—one syllable

which	whisk	_____
whiff	whit	_____
whim	whiz	_____
whip	_____	_____

WHI /ʍɪ/—two syllables

whicker	whipsaw	whither
whiffle	whipsnake	whittle
whimper	whipstitch	whittling
whimsy	whisker	whiz-bang
whinny	whisper	whizzer
whipcord	whistle	_____
whiplash	whistler	_____
whippet	whistling	_____

YI /jɪ/—one syllable
yip

YI /jɪ/—two syllables
yippee

ZI /zɪ/—one syllable

zig	zinc	zip
zilch	zing	zit

ZI /zɪ/—two syllables

xiphoid	zincite	zippy
zigzag	zinger	zither
zillion	zingy	_____
zincic	zipper	_____

IB /ɪb/—final

bib	gib	rib
crib	glib	sib
dib	jib	_____
fib	nib	_____

ICH /ɪtʃ/—final

ditch	rich	witch
glitch	snitch	_____
hitch	stitch	_____
itch	switch	_____
niche	twitch	_____
pitch	which	_____

ILCH /ɪltʃ/—final

filch	zilch	_____

INCH /ɪntʃ/—final

chinch	finch	pinch
cinch	flinch	winch
clinch	inch	_____

ID /ɪd/—final

bid	id	rid
did	kid	skid
grid	lid	slid
hid	mid	squid

ILD /ɪld/—final

billed	grilled	thrilled
build	guild	tilled
chilled	killed	trilled
drilled	milled	twilled
filled	quilled	willed
frilled	skilled	_____
gild	spilled	_____
gilled	stilled	_____

IMD /ɪmd/—final

brimmed	rimmed	slimmed
dimmed	skimmed	trimmed

IND /ɪnd/—final

chinned	shinned	twinned
finned	sinned	wind
ginned	skinned	_____
grinned	thinned	_____
pinned	tinned	_____

IF /ɪf/—final

cliff	riff	tiff
if	skiff	whiff
miff	stiff	_____

IMF /ɪmf/—final

lymph	_____	_____
nymph	_____	_____

IG /ɪg/—final

big	pig	zig
brig	prig	_____
dig	rig	_____
fig	sprig	_____
gig	twig	_____
jig	wig	_____

IK /ɪk/—final

brick	lick	stick
chick	nick	thick
click	pick	tic
crick	quick	tick
flick	rick	trick
hick	sick	wick
kick	slick	_____

ILK /ɪlk/—final

bilk	milk	_____
ilk	silk	_____

ISK /ɪsk/—final

bisque	frisk	whisk
brisk	risk	_____
disk	tsk	_____

IL /ɪl/—final

bill	kill	skill
chill	krill	spill
dill	mil	still
drill	mill	thrill
fill	nil	till
frill	pill	trill
gill	quill	twill
grill	rill	will
hill	shrill	_____
ill	sill	_____

IM /ɪm/—final

brim	limb	vim
dim	rim	whim
glim	skim	_____
grim	slim	_____
gym	swim	_____
him	trim	_____

IN /ɪn/—final

been	inn	thin
bin	kin	tin
chin	pin	twin
din	shin	win
fin	sin	_____
grin	skin	_____
in	spin	_____

ING /ɪŋ/—final

bring	ring	thing
cling	sing	ting
ding	sling	wing
fling	spring	wring
king	sting	zing
ling	string	_____
ping	swing	_____

INK /ɪŋk/—final

blink	link	slink
brink	mink	stink
chink	pink	sync
clink	rink	think
drink	shrink	twink
ink	sink	wink
kink	skink	zinc

IP /ɪp/—final

blip	kip	skip
chip	lip	slip
clip	nip	snip
dip	pip	strip
drip	quip	tip
flip	rip	trip
grip	scrip	whip
gyp	ship	yip
hip	sip	zip

IMP /ɪmp/—final

blimp	limp	skimp
chimp	primp	wimp
crimp	scrimp	_____
imp	shrimp	_____

IS /ɪs/—final

bliss	kiss	sis
hiss	miss	this

IKS /ɪks/—final

bricks	licks	ticks
chicks	mix	tricks
clicks	nix	wicks
cricks	picks	_____
fix	ricks	_____
flicks	six	_____
kicks	sticks	_____

INKS /ɪŋks/—final

chinks	plinks	thinks
drinks	rinks	winks
jinx	shrinks	_____
kinks	sinks	_____
links	skinks	_____
lynx	slinks	_____
minx	stinks	_____

INS /ɪns/—final

mince	quince	since
prince	rinse	wince

INTS /ɪnts/—final

blintze	hints	sprints
chintz	mints	squints
flints	prints	tints
glints	splints	_____

ISH /ɪʃ/—final

dish	squish	wish
fish	swish	_____

IT /ɪt/—final

bit	knit	snit
chit	lit	spit
dit	mitt	split
fit	nit	twit
flit	pit	wit
grit	quit	zit
hit	sit	_____
it	skit	_____
kit	slit	_____

IFT /ɪft/—final

drift	rift	swift
gift	shift	thrift
lift	shrift	_____
miffed	sift	_____

IKST /ɪkst/—final

fixed	nixed	_____
mixed	twixt	_____

ILT /ɪlt/—final

built	lilt	tilt
guilt	quilt	wilt
hilt	silt	_____
jilt	spilt	_____
kilt	stilt	_____

INT /ɪnt/—final

dint	lint	sprint
flint	mint	squint
glint	print	stint
hint	splint	tint

IPT /ɪpt/—final

chipped	quipped	tipped
clipped	ripped	tripped
crypt	script	whipped
dipped	shipped	yipped
dripped	sipped	zipped
flipped	skipped	_____
gripped	slipped	_____
gypped	snipped	_____
lipped	stripped	_____

IST /ɪst/—final

fist	kissed	schist
gist	list	twist
grist	missed	wrist
hissed	mist	_____

ITH /ɪð/—final

with	_____	_____

ITH /ɪθ/—final

kith	smith	_____
pith	with	_____

ILTH /ɪlθ/—final

filth	_____	_____

INTH /ɪnθ/—final

plinth	_____	_____

IV /ɪv/—final

give	live	sieve

IZ /ɪz/—final

fizz	his	quiz
frizz	is	whiz

O /o/

O /o/—one syllable

oak	ode	old
oat	oh	owe
oath	ohm	own

O /o/—two syllables

oaken	olden	opine
oatcake	older	opus
oatmeal	oldie	otic
obese	oldish	oval
obey	oldness	ovate
oboe	omen	over
ocean	omit	overt
ocher	only	ovine
odor	onus	ovoid
ogre	opal	owing
okay	opaque	owner
okra	open	ozone

BO /bo/—one syllable

beau	bole	bogue
boast	boll	both
boat	bolt	bow
bode	bone	bowed
bold	boned	bowl

BO /bo/—two syllables

boa	boathouse	bogey
boaster	boating	bogus
boastful	boatload	bolder
boater	boatyard	boldface

O

boldly	boneless	bovine
boldness	boner	bowler
bollworm	bonus	bowlful
bolo	bony	bowline
bolster	boulder	bowling
bone-dry	bouquet	bowstring

CHO /tʃo/—one syllable

choke	chose	_____

CHO /tʃo/—two syllables

choker	choky	chosen

DO /do/—one syllable

doe	don't	dough
dole	dose	dove
dome	dote	doze

DO /do/—two syllables

docent	doleful	dotage
dodo	domain	doughnut
doeskin	donate	doughy
dogie	donor	dozer
dojo	dosage	_____

FO /fo/—one syllable

foal	foe	folk
foam	fold	phone

FO /fo/—two syllables

foamy	foldless	phoneme
focal	folklore	phony
foci	folksy	photic
focus	folkway	photo
foldboat	foment	_____
folder	phobic	_____
folding	phonate	_____

GO /go/—one syllable

ghost	goal	gold
go	goat	_____
goad	goes	_____

GO /go/—two syllables

ghostlike	goatskin	goldfish
ghostly	go-cart	goldsmith
ghostwrite	goer	gopher
goalie	gofer	_____
goatee	going	_____
goatherd	golden	_____

HO /ho/—one syllable

ho	hole	hose
hoax	home	host
hoe	hone	whole
hold	hope	_____

HO /ho/—two syllables

hoagie	holy	homey
hoaxer	homebound	homing
hobo	homeland	hopeful
hocus	homeless	hopeless
hoedown	homely	hoping
hogan	homemade	hostess
ho-hum	homer	hotel
hokey	homeroom	wholesale
hokum	homesick	wholesome
holder	homesite	whole-wheat
holding	homestead	wholly
holdout	hometown	_____
holey	homeward	_____
holster	homework	_____

JO /dʒo/—one syllable

joke	jolt	_____

O

JO /dʒo/ —two syllables

jocose	joker	_____
jocund	jolter	_____
joey	jolty	_____

KO /ko/ —one syllable

coach	code	cote
coak	cold	cove
coal	colt	kohl
coast	comb	_____
coat	cone	_____
coax	cope	_____

KO /ko/ —two syllables

coacher	coesite	coquille
coact	cogent	coset
coaly	coheir	cosign
coaming	cohere	cosine
coastal	coho	co-star
coaster	cohort	cosy
coastline	co-host	covert
coastward	cola	cowrite
coastwise	colder	kola
coated	coldest	kopek
coating	coldly	kosher
coatrack	coldness	_____
coatroom	cold-pack	_____
coattail	coleslaw	_____
coaxer	collate	_____
cobalt	colon	_____
cobra	colter	_____
cocoa	coltish	_____
coda	coma	_____
coded	comber	_____
coder	co-op	_____
coding	coping	_____
coerce	copra	

LO /lo/ —one syllable

lo	loathe	loge
load	loaves	lone
loaf	lobe	lope
loam	lobed	low
loan	lode	_____

LO /lo/ —two syllables

loaded	locus	lotion
loader	locust	lotus
loading	lodestar	lowboy
loafer	lodestone	low-cost
loamy	logo	lower
loaner	loma	low-grade
loathing	loment	low-key
local	lonely	lowland
locale	loner	lowly
locate	lonesome	_____
loci	loquat	_____

MO /mo/ —one syllable

mauve	mold	mote
moan	mole	mould
moat	molt	mow
mode	mope	mown
mol	most	_____

MO /mo/ —two syllables

mobile	molding	mosey
mocha	moldy	mostly
modal	molehill	motel
modem	moleskin	motif
modish	molten	motile
mogul	molter	motion
mohair	moment	motive
molar	moped	motor
molder	moper	mower

NO /no/—one syllable

gnome	known	nope
knoll	no	nose
know	node	note

NO /no/—two syllables

gnomish	no-how	notepad
know-how	nomad	notice
knowing	nosebleed	notion
noble	nosedive	nova
nobly	nosepiece	nowhere
nodal	nosy	no-win
no-fault	notate	_____
no-go	notebook	_____
no-hit	noted	_____

PO /po/—one syllable

poach	poll	pope
poke	pome	pose
pole	pone	post

PO /po/—two syllables

poacher	polo	postmark
poem	pony	postpone
poet	postage	postscript
poker	postal	posy
poky	postbox	potent
polar	postcard	potion
polecat	postdate	poultice
pole-vault	poster	poultry
polka	posthole	_____
pollster	posting	_____

RO /ro/—one syllable

roach	roan	rode
road	roast	roe
roam	robe	rogue

role	rose	_____
roll	rote	_____
rolled	rove	_____
rope	row	_____
roque	wrote	_____

RO /ro/—two syllables

roadbed	roguish	rosette
roadblock	role-play	rosewood
roadhouse	rollback	rosy
roadside	roller	rotate
roadster	rolling	rotor
roadway	rollout	rotund
roadwork	romaine	rover
roamer	romance	roving
roaster	roper	rowboat
roasting	roping	rower
robot	roquet	_____
robust	rosebud	_____
rodent	rosebush	_____

SO /so/—one syllable

sew	soap	soul
sewn	sold	sow
so	sole	_____
soak	sone	_____

SO /so/—two syllables

sewing	soda	sonar
soakage	sofa	so-so
soaker	sojourn	soulful
soapbox	solar	soulless
soapstone	soldier	sower
soapsuds	solely	_____
soapy	soli	_____
sober	solo	_____
social	solstice	_____

O

SHO /ʃo/—one syllable

shoal	shone	shown
shoat	show	_____

SHO /ʃo/—two syllables

chauffeur	showdown	showplace
shoulder	showing	showroom
showboat	show-off	showy
showcase	showpiece	_____

TO /to/—one syllable

taupe	told	tote
toad	toll	tow
toast	tome	_____
toe	tone	_____

TO /to/—two syllables

toady	toller	totem
toaster	toll-free	towage
toasty	tollgate	towboat
toehold	tollhouse	towhead
toenail	tollway	towhee
tofu	tonal	towline
toga	toner	towpath
tokay	tonette	towrope
token	topaz	towy
tollbooth	total	_____

THO /ðo/—one syllable

tho	those	though

THO /θo/—one syllable

thole	_____	_____

VO /vo/—one syllable

vogue	volt	_____
vole	vote	_____

VO /vo/—two syllables

vocal	voltage	_____
volant	voter	_____
volar	votive	_____

WO /wo/—one syllable

woad	woke	won't
woe	wold	wove

WO /wo/—two syllables

woaded	woven	_____
woeful	_____	_____

YO /jo/—one syllable

yoke	_____	_____
yolk	_____	_____

YO /jo/—two syllables

yeoman	yodel	yogurt
yeomen	yoga	yokel

ZO /zo/—one syllable

zone	zoned	_____

ZO /zo/—two syllables

zonal	zoning	_____
zonate	zonule	_____
zoneless	zooid	_____

O /o/—final

beau	foe	lo
blow	glow	low
bow	go	mow
crow	grow	no
doe	ho	oh
dough	hoe	owe
flow	know	pro

roe	so	tow
row	sow	woe
sew	stow	_____
show	though	_____
slow	throw	_____
snow	toe	_____

OB /ob/—final

globe	probe	strobe
lobe	robe	_____

OCH /otʃ/—final

broach	coach	roach
brooch	poach	_____

OD /od/—final

bode	lode	sewed
bowed	mode	showed
code	mowed	slowed
crowed	node	snowed
glowed	ode	strode
goad	owed	toad
hoed	road	woad
load	rode	_____

OLD /old/—final

bold	mold	scold
cold	mould	scrolled
fold	old	sold
gold	polled	told
hold	rolled	trolled

OND /ond/—final

boned	loaned	toned
cloned	moaned	zoned
groaned	owned	_____
honed	phoned	

OF /of/—final

loaf   _____   _____

OG /og/—final

| bogue | rogue | _____ |
| brogue | vogue | _____ |

OK /ok/—final

bloke	joke	stoke
broke	oak	stroke
choke	poke	woke
cloak	roque	yoke
coak	smoke	yolk
croak	soak	_____
folk	spoke	_____

OL /ol/—final

bole	knoll	soul
boll	mole	stole
bowl	pole	stroll
coal	poll	toll
dole	role	troll
droll	roll	vole
foal	scroll	whole
goal	shoal	_____
hole	sole	

OM /om/—final

chrome	gloam	ohm
comb	gnome	pome
dome	home	roam
foam	loam	tome

ON /on/—final

blown	cone	groan
bone	drone	grown
clone	flown	hone

known	prone	stone
loan	roan	throne
lone	sewn	tone
moan	scone	zone
own	shone	_____
phone	shown	_____
pone	sone	_____

OP /op/—final

cope	mope	scope
grope	nope	slope
hope	pope	soap
lope	rope	taupe

OS /os/—final

close	dose	gross

OKS /oks/—final

blokes	hoax	strokes
chokes	jokes	yokes
cloaks	oaks	_____
coax	pokes	_____
croaks	soaks	_____
folks	spokes	_____

OT /ot/—final

bloat	moat	stoat
boat	mote	throat
coat	note	tote
dote	oat	vote
float	quote	wrote
gloat	rote	_____
goat	shoat	_____

OLT /olt/—final

bolt	jolt	smolt
colt	molt	volt

ONT /ont/—final
won't _____ _____

OST /ost/—final

boast	grossed	post
coast	host	roast
ghost	most	toast

OTH /oð/—final

clothe	loathe	_____

OTH /oθ/—final

both	growth	oath

OV /ov/—final

clove	grove	strove
cove	mauve	throve
dove	rove	trove
drove	stove	wove

O

OZ /oz/—final

chose	goes	slows
close	grows	snows
crows	hose	stows
doze	nose	those
flows	pose	throws
froze	prose	_____
glows	rose	_____
gloze	shows	_____

OZH /oʒ/—final
loge _____ _____

O /ɒ/

O /ɒ/ — **one syllable**

odd	on	ox
odds	opt	_____

O /ɒ/ — **two syllables**

honest	oddish	optic
honor	oddly	option
object	oddment	osprey
oblate	oddness	otter
oblong	olive	oxcart
obverse	omelette	oxen
obvert	onrush	oxtail
octad	onshore	_____
octane	onside	_____
octant	onstage	_____
octave	onto	_____
octet	onward	_____
odder	onyx	_____

BO /bɒ/ — **one syllable**

bob	bop	box
bog	bosh	_____
bond	boss	_____
bonk	botch	_____

BO /bɒ/ — **two syllables**

bobber	bobtail	boggy
bobbin	bobwhite	bombard
bobble	bodice	bonbon
bobcat	body	bondage
bobsled	boggle	bonded

bonfire	bother	boxer
bongo	bottle	boxful
bonnet	bottled	boxing
bonsai	bottom	boxwood
bonspiel	boxball	_____
botchy	boxcar	_____

CHO /tʃɒ/ —one syllable

chock	chomp	chop

CHO /tʃɒ/ —two syllables

chocolate	chopping	chopsticks
chopper	choppy	

DO /dɒ/ —one syllable

dock	dog	dot
dodge	doll	_____
doff	don	_____

DO /dɒ/ —two syllables

dobber	dockyard	dollhouse
dobbin	doctor	dollop
dobby	doctrine	dolly
docile	dodder	dolphin
dockage	dodger	donkey
docker	doffer	dosser
docket	doghouse	_____
dockside	dollar	_____

FO /fɒ/ —one syllable

fob	fond	fox
fog	font	_____

FO /fɒ/ —two syllables

fodder	foggy	folly
fogbound	foghorn	fondant
fogger	follow	fondly

fondness	fox-fire	fox-trot
fondue	foxglove	foxy
fossil	foxhound	phonic

GO /gɒ/—one syllable

gob	gong	got
golf	gosh	_____

GO /gɒ/—two syllables

gobbet	godlike	goshawk
gobble	godly	gosling
gobbler	godsend	gospel
goblet	goffer	gossip
goblin	goggle	gotten
godchild	golfer	_____
goddess	golly	_____
godless	goner	_____

HO /hɒ/—one syllable

hob	hog	hot
hock	honk	hotch
hod	hop	_____

HO /hɒ/—two syllables

hobble	hollow	hostile
hobby	holly	hotchpotch
hobnail	homage	hothouse
hobnob	honker	hotly
hockey	hopper	hotshot
hockle	hopping	hotter
hockshop	hopscotch	hotwork
hodgepodge	hostage	_____
holler	hostel	_____

JO /dʒɒ/—one syllable

job	jog	_____
jock	jot	_____

JO /dʒɒ/—two syllables

jobber	jogging	jotter
jobless	joggle	jotting
jockey	jolly	_____
jocund	jonquil	_____
jodhpurs	jostle	_____
jogger	jotted	_____

KO /kɒ/—one syllable

cob	con	cop
cod	conch	cot
cog	conk	_____

KO /kɒ/—two syllables

cobble	column	condo
cobbler	combat	condor
cobweb	combine	conduct
cockboat	comet	confab
cocker	comfit	conflict
cockeyed	comic	conjure
cockle	comma	conquer
cockpit	comment	conquest
cockroach	commerce	conscious
cockspur	common	console
cocksure	commune	consul
cocky	compact	contact
coddle	compost	content
codfish	compound	contest
codger	comrade	context
cognate	concave	contour
cogwheel	concept	contract
colic	concert	contrast
collar	conclave	convent
collard	concoct	convex
collate	concord	convict
college	concourse	convoy
collie	concrete	copper

O

copra	cosset	cotton
copter	costly	coxswain
copy	costume	_____
cosmic	cottage	_____
cosmos	cotter	_____

LO /lɒ/—one syllable

lob	lodge	lot
loch	loll	lox
lock	lop	_____

LO /lɒ/—two syllables

lobber	locket	lodgment
lobby	lockout	logic
lobster	locksmith	lopping
lockage	lockup	lotto
lockbox	lodger	lozenge
locker	lodging	_____

MO /mɒ/—one syllable

mock	mom	mosque
mod	mop	_____

MO /mɒ/—two syllables

mocker	monarch	moppet
model	mongoose	mop-up
modern	mongrel	motley
modest	monsoon	mottle
module	monster	motto
mollusk	monstrous	moxie
momma	montage	_____
mommy	mopboard	_____

NO /nɒ/—one syllable

knob	nob	nog
knock	nock	not
knot	nod	notch

NO /nɒ/—two syllables

knobby	nocturn	nostril
knockdown	nocturne	notchy
knocker	nodding	novel
knockout	nodule	novice
knockwurst	noggin	noxious
knothole	nogging	nozzle
knotted	nonfat	_____
knotter	nonplus	_____
knotting	nonsense	_____
knotty	nonskid	_____
knowledge	nonstick	_____
nobby	nonstop	

PO /pɒ/—one syllable

pock	pond	pox
pod	pons	_____
podge	pop	_____
pomp	posh	_____

PO /pɒ/—two syllables

pocket	pontiff	potash
pockmark	pontine	pothole
polish	pontoon	potlatch
pollen	popcorn	potluck
polyp	poplar	potpie
pommel	poplin	potter
pompon	poppy	_____
pompous	pop-up	_____
poncho	posit	_____
ponder	possum	_____
pongee	posture	_____

RO /rɒ/—one syllable

rob	romp	_____
rock	rot	_____
rod	_____	_____

O

RO /rɒ/ —two syllables

robber	roger	rostrum
robin	rollick	rotten
rocker	romper	_____
rocket	rompish	_____
rockfish	rondeau	_____
rockwork	rosin	_____
rocky	roster	_____

SO /sɒ/ —one syllable

sob	solve	sox
sock	song	_____
sod	sop	_____

SO /sɒ/ —two syllables

sobbing	solemn	sonnet
soccer	solid	sopping
socket	solstice	soppy
sodden	solute	_____
soggy	solvent	_____
solace	somber	_____
solder	sonic	_____

SHO /ʃɒ/ —one syllable

shock	shop	_____
shod	shot	_____

SHO /ʃɒ/ —two syllables

shocker	shoplift	shopworn
shocking	shopper	_____
shockproof	shopping	_____
shoddy	shoptalk	_____

TO /tɒ/ —one syllable

tock	top	_____
tog	tops	_____
tom	tot	_____

TO /tɒ/ —two syllables

tocsin	topcoat	topside
toddle	topic	topsoil
toddler	topknot	totter
toggle	topline	toxic
tomcat	topmost	toxin
tonic	topnotch	toxoid
tonsil	topper	_____
tonsure	topping	_____
tontine	topple	_____

VO /vɒ/ —two syllables

volley	volume	vomit

WO /wɒ/ —one syllable

wad	wash	wok
wand	wasp	_____
want	watch	_____
was	watt	_____

WO /wɒ/ —two syllables

wadding	washer	watcher
waddle	washing	watchful
waffle	washout	watchword
wallet	washrag	wattage
wallow	washroom	wattle
wander	washtub	wobble
wanting	wasn't	wobbling
washboard	waspish	wobbly
washbowl	watchband	wombat
washcloth	watchdog	_____

WHO /ʍɒ/ —one syllable

whop	_____	_____

WHO /ʍɒ/ —two syllables

whopper	whopping	_____

O

YO /jɒ/—one syllable

yacht	yon	_____

YO /jɒ/—two syllables

yachting	yonder	_____

OB /ɒb/—final

blob	hob	slob
bob	job	snob
cob	knob	sob
fob	lob	squab
glob	mob	swab
gob	nob	throb

OCH /ɒtʃ/—final

blotch	hotch	splotch
botch	notch	swatch
crotch	scotch	watch

ONCH /ɒntʃ/—final

conch	_____	_____

OD /ɒd/—final

clod	plod	sod
cod	pod	squad
hod	prod	trod
mod	quad	wad
nod	rod	_____
odd	shod	_____

OND /ɒnd/—final

blond	donned	pond
bond	fond	wand
conned	frond	_____

OF /ɒf/—final

doff	quaff	_____

OLF /ɒlf/—**final**

golf _____ _____

OG /ɒg/—**final**

bog	frog	tog
clog	hog	_____
cog	jog	_____
dog	log	_____
flog	nog	_____
fog	smog	_____

OJ /ɒdʒ/—**final**

dodge lodge _____

OK /ɒk/—**final**

block	jock	smock
chock	knock	sock
clock	lock	stock
crock	mock	tock
dock	nock	wok
flock	pock	_____
frock	rock	_____
hock	shock	_____

ONK /ɒŋk/—**final**

bonk conk honk

OSK /ɒsk/—**final**

mosque _____ _____

OL /ɒl/—**final**

doll	_____	_____
loll	_____	_____

OM /ɒm/—**final**

from	prom	_____
mom	tom	_____

O

ON /ɒn/ —final

con	on	swan
don	scone	yon

OP /ɒp/ —final

bop	hop	sop
chop	lop	stop
clop	mop	strop
cop	plop	swap
crop	pop	swop
drop	prop	top
flop	shop	whop

OMP /ɒmp/ —final

chomp	romp	trompe
clomp	stomp	whomp
pomp	swamp	_____

OSP /ɒsp/ —final

wasp	_____	_____

OS /ɒs/ —final

dross	gloss	_____

OKS /ɒks/ —final

box	hocks	rocks
chocks	knocks	shocks
clocks	locks	smocks
crocks	lox	socks
docks	mocks	sox
flocks	ox	stocks
fox	phlox	_____
frocks	pox	_____

OSH /ɒʃ/ —final

bosh	slosh	swash
posh	squash	wash

OT /ɒt/—final

blot	lot	swat
clot	not	tot
cot	plot	trot
dot	rot	watt
got	shot	what
hot	slot	yacht
jot	spot	_____
knot	squat	_____

ONT /ɒnt/—final

font	want	_____

OPT /ɒpt/—final

chopped	lopped	sopped
clopped	mopped	stopped
cropped	opt	stropped
dropped	popped	swapped
flopped	propped	topped
glopped	shopped	_____
hopped	slopped	_____

OTH /ɒθ/—final

swath	_____	_____

OLV /ɒlv/—final

solve	_____	_____

OZ /ɒz/—final

was	_____	_____

ONZ /ɒnz/—final

bronze	dons	scones
cons	pons	swans

O

O /ɔ/

O /ɔ/ — one syllable

all	awe	ought
aught	off	_____
auk	oft	_____

O /ɔ/ — two syllables

alder	augment	offer
all-out	august	offhand
all-star	auklet	offhour
almost	auspice	office
also	austere	off-key
altar	author	off-line
alter	auto	off-load
although	autumn	offshoot
always	awesome	offshore
auburn	awestruck	offside
auction	awful	off-stage
audit	awkward	off-white
augend	awning	often
auger	offbeat	ostrich

BO /bɔ/ — one syllable

bald	baud	boss
balk	bawl	bought
ball	bog	_____

BO /bɔ/ — two syllables

baldness	balsa	bawler
balker	balsam	bossy
balky	bauble	_____
ballpark	bauxite	_____

134

CHO /tʃɔ/ —**one syllable**
chalk   _____   _____

CHO /tʃɔ/ —**two syllables**

chalkboard	chalky	chocolate

DO /dɔ/ —**one syllable**

daub	dawk	dog
daunt	dawn	_____

DO /dɔ/ —**two syllables**

daughter	dawning	doggy
dauntless	dogcart	doghouse
dawdle	dog-ear	dogma
dawdler	doggone	dogwood

FO /fɔ/ —**one syllable**

fall	faun	fought
false	fawn	_____
fault	fog	_____

FO /fɔ/ —**two syllables**

falcon	falsely	fauna
fallback	falseness	fogbound
fallen	falter	fogger
falloff	faucet	foggy
fallout	faultless	foghorn
falsehood	faulty	foster

GO /gɔ/ —**one syllable**

gall	gauze	gong
gaud	gawk	_____
gaunt	gone	_____

GO /gɔ/ —**two syllables**

gallstone	gauntlet	gawky
gaudy	gauzy	goner

O

HO /hɔ/—one syllable

hall	haunch	hawk
halt	haunt	hawse
haul	haw	hog

HO /hɔ/—two syllables

hallmark	haunter	hog-tie
hallway	haunting	hogwash
halter	hawker	hogweed
haughty	hawking	_____
haulage	hawthorn	_____
hauler	hoggish	_____
haunted	hogpen	_____

JO /dʒɔ/—one syllable

jaunt	_____	_____
jaw	_____	_____

JO /dʒɔ/—two syllables

jaundice	jawbone	_____
jaunty	jawless	_____

KO /kɔ/—one syllable

calk	cause	cough
call	caw	_____
caught	cog	_____
caulk	cost	_____

KO /kɔ/—two syllables

calker	caulker	coffin
callback	causal	costly
call-board	causeway	cougher
caller	caustic	_____
call-in	caution	_____
calling	cautious	_____
caucus	coffee	_____
cauldron	coffer	_____

LO /lɔ/ —**one syllable**

laud	loft	loss
launch	log	lost
law	logged	_____
lawn	long	_____

LO /lɔ/ —**two syllables**

launcher	logger	long-range
launder	logging	longshore
laundry	logjam	long-term
lawbook	logroll	long-time
lawful	longboat	longways
lawsuit	longer	longwise
lawyer	longhand	_____
lofty	longing	_____
logbook	long-lived	_____

MO /mɔ/ —**one syllable**

mall	maud	moss
malt	maul	moth

MO /mɔ/ —**two syllables**

malted	mossy	mothy
maudlin	mothball	_____
maunder	mothproof	_____

NO /nɔ/ —**one syllable**

gnaw	nautch	_____
naught	_____	_____

NO /nɔ/ —**two syllables**

gnawer	naughty	_____
gnawing	nauseous	_____

PO /pɔ/ —**one syllable**

pall	pause	pawl
paunch	paw	pawn

PO /pɔ/—two syllables

palsy	papaw	_____
palter	pauper	_____
paltry	pawnshop	_____

RO /rɔ/—one syllable

raw	wroth	_____
wrong	wrought	_____

RO /rɔ/—two syllables

raucous	rawhide	wrongful
rawboned	rawness	wrongly

SO /sɔ/—one syllable

salt	saw	song
sauce	soft	sought

SO /sɔ/—two syllables

salted	sawing	softest
saltine	sawmill	softly
salty	saw-toothed	software
saucepan	sawyer	softwood
saucer	softball	softy
saucy	soft-boiled	songbird
sawdust	softbound	songfest
sawfish	soften	_____
sawhorse	softer	_____

SHO /ʃɔ/—one syllable

shaw	_____	_____
shawl	_____	_____

TO /tɔ/—one syllable

talk	taut	toss
tall	taw	tossed
taught	tong	_____
taunt	tongs	_____

TO /tɔ/—two syllables

talker	taurine	tawny
talking	tautly	toffee
taller	tautness	tossup
tallest	tawdry	_____

THO /θɔ/—one syllable

thaw	thong	thought

THO /θɔ/—two syllables

thoughtful	_____	_____

VO /vɔ/—one syllable

vault	vaunt	_____

VO /vɔ/—two syllables

vaudeville	vaulter	_____
vaulted	vaulting	_____

WO /wɔ/—one syllable

walk	walled	_____
wall	waltz	_____

WO /wɔ/—two syllables

walker	walkway	walrus
walk-in	wallboard	water
walking	wallet	watered
walkout	walleye	_____
walk-through	walnut	_____

YO /jɔ/—one syllable

yaw	yawn	_____
yawl	yawp	_____

YO /jɔ/—two syllables

yawner	yawning	_____
yawnful	yawny	_____

O

O /ɔ/ —final

awe	haw	straw
caw	jaw	taw
claw	law	thaw
craw	paw	yaw
daw	raw	_____
draw	saw	_____
flaw	slaw	_____
gnaw	squaw	_____

OB /ɔb/ —final

daub	_____	_____

OCH /ɔtʃ/ —final

nautch	_____	_____

ONCH /ɔntʃ/ —final

haunch	staunch	_____
launch	_____	_____
paunch	_____	_____

OD /ɔd/ —final

awed	gaud	tawed
baud	gnawed	thawed
broad	hawed	yawed
cawed	laud	_____
clawed	maud	_____
flawed	pawed	_____
fraud	sawed	_____

OLD /ɔld/ —final

bald	hauled	squalled
balled	mauled	stalled
bawled	palled	trawled
called	scald	walled
crawled	scrawled	_____
drawled	sprawled	_____

OF /ɔf/—final

cough	quaff	_____
doff	scoff	_____
off	trough	_____

OG /ɔg/—final

bog	fog	hog
dog	frog	log

OK /ɔk/—final

auk	dawk	talk
balk	gawk	walk
calk	hawk	_____
caulk	squawk	_____
chalk	stalk	_____

O

OL /ɔl/—final

all	haul	tall
ball	mall	thrall
bawl	maul	trawl
brawl	pall	wall
call	scrawl	yawl
crawl	shawl	_____
drawl	small	_____
fall	sprawl	_____
gall	squall	_____
hall	stall	_____

OM /ɔm/—final

qualm	_____	_____

ON /ɔn/—final

brawn	lawn	yawn
dawn	pawn	_____
drawn	prawn	_____
fawn	sawn	_____
gone	spawn	_____

ONG /ɔŋ/ —final

gong	strong	wrong
long	thong	_____
prong	throng	_____
song	tong	_____

OS /ɔs/ —final

boss	loss	_____
cross	moss	_____
floss	sauce	_____
gloss	toss	_____

OT /ɔt/ —final

aught	naught	wrought
bought	ought	_____
brought	sought	_____
caught	taught	_____
fought	taut	_____
fraught	thought	_____

OFT /ɔft/ —final

coughed	doffed	soft
croft	loft	_____

OLT /ɔlt/ —final

fault	malt	vault
halt	salt	_____

ONT /ɔnt/ —final

daunt	jaunt	_____
flaunt	taunt	_____
gaunt	vaunt	_____
haunt	_____	_____

OST /ɔst/ —final

cost	frost	tossed
crossed	lost	_____

OTH /ɔθ/—final

broth	moth	troth
cloth	sloth	wroth
froth	swath	_____

OZ /ɔz/—final

cause	flaws	pause
caws	gauze	saws
clause	gnaws	squaws
claws	hawse	straws
daws	jaws	thaws
draws	laws	_____

O

OI /ɔɪ/

OI /ɔɪ/ — one syllable

oil	oy	_____
oink	_____	_____

OI /ɔɪ/ — two syllables

oilcan	oiler	oily
oilcloth	oilseed	ointment
oilcup	oilstone	oyster

BOI /bɔɪ/ — one syllable

boil	buoy	_____
boy	_____	_____

BOI /bɔɪ/ — two syllables

boiler	boyfriend	buoyant
boiling	boyhood	_____
boycott	boyish	_____

CHOI /tʃɔɪ/ — one syllable

choice	choil	_____

CHOI /tʃɔɪ/ — two syllables

choiceless	choiceness	_____
choicely	choicer	_____

DOI /dɔɪ/ — one syllable

doit	_____	_____

DOI /dɔɪ/ — two syllables

doily	doitkin	doyenne
doited	doyen	_____

144

FOI /fɔɪ/—**one syllable**

foil   foist   _____

FOI /fɔɪ/—**two syllables**

foible   foyer   _____
foiling   _____   _____

GOI /gɔɪ/—**two syllables**

goiter   goitrous   _____

HOI /hɔɪ/—**one syllable**

hoise   hoy   _____
hoist   _____   _____

HOI /hɔɪ/—**two syllables**

hoisted   hoister   _____

JOI /dʒɔɪ/—**one syllable**

join   joist   _____
joint   joy   _____

JOI /dʒɔɪ/—**two syllables**

joinder   jointless   joyless
joiner   jointly   joyous
jointed   jointure   joy-ride
jointer   joyful   _____

KOI /kɔɪ/—**one syllable**

coif   coiled   coy
coil   coin   _____

KOI /kɔɪ/—**two syllables**

coinage   coyish   coyness
coiner   coyly   _____

LOI /lɔɪ/—**one syllable**

loin   _____   _____

O

LOI /lɔɪ/—two syllables

lawyer	loiter	_____
loincloth	loyal	_____

MOI /mɔɪ/—one syllable

moil	moist	moit

MOI /mɔɪ/—two syllables

moisten	moistness	_____
moister	moisture	_____
moistless	moity	_____

NOI /nɔɪ/—one syllable

noil	noise	_____

NOI /nɔɪ/—two syllables

noiseless	noisome	_____
noiseproof	noisy	_____

POI /pɔɪ/—one syllable

poi	point	_____
poil	poise	_____

POI /pɔɪ/—two syllables

poignant	pointer	pointy
point-blank	pointing	poiser
pointed	pointless	poison

ROI /rɔɪ/—one syllable

roil	_____	_____

ROI /rɔɪ/—two syllables

roily	royal	_____
roister	royale	_____

SOI /sɔɪ/—one syllable

soil	soy	_____

SOI /sɔɪ/—two syllables

soilage	soilure	soybean
soiling	soya	_____

TOI /tɔɪ/—one syllable

toil	toy	_____

TOI /tɔɪ/—two syllables

toiler	toilsome	toyshop
toilet	toilworn	_____
toilful	toyer	_____

VOI /vɔɪ/—one syllable

voice	void	_____
voiced	voile	_____

VOI /vɔɪ/—two syllables

voiceful	voicing	voider
voiceless	voidance	voyage
voiceprint	voided	_____

YOI /jɔɪ/—one syllable

yoicks	_____	_____

OI /ɔɪ/—final

boy	joy	soy
cloy	oy	toy
coy	ploy	troy
hoy	poi	_____

OID /ɔɪd/—final

toyed	void	_____

OILD /ɔɪld/—final

boiled	foiled	soiled
broiled	oiled	spoiled
coiled	roiled	toiled

O

OIF /ɔɪf/—final
coif   _____   _____

OIL /ɔɪl/—final

boil	noil	spoil
broil	oil	toil
coil	poil	voile
foil	roil	_____
moil	soil	_____

OIN /ɔɪn/—final

coin	join	quoin
groin	loin	_____

OINK /ɔɪŋk/—final
oink   _____   _____

OIS /ɔɪs/—final

choice	voice	_____

OIKS /ɔɪks/—final
yoicks   _____   _____

OIT /ɔɪt/—final

doit	moit	quoit

OINT /ɔɪnt/—final

joint	point	_____

OIST /ɔɪst/—final

foist	joist	voiced
hoist	moist	_____

OIZ /ɔɪz/—final

boys	noise	toys
cloys	ploys	_____
joys	poise	_____

OU /aʊ/

OU /aʊ/ — one syllable

ouch	oust	owl
ounce	out	_____

OU /aʊ/ — two syllables

ouster	outgrew	outrun
outage	outgrowth	outshine
outbid	outhouse	outside
outboard	outing	outsmart
outbound	outlast	outthink
outcome	outlaw	outward
outcry	outlet	outwear
outdo	outline	outwit
outdoor	outlook	outworn
outer	outpost	owlet
outfield	outpour	_____
outfit	output	_____
outfox	outreach	_____
outgo	outright	_____

BOU /baʊ/ — one syllable

bough	bound	bout
bounce	bounds	bow

BOU /baʊ/ — two syllables

boughless	bounded	bowel
bouncing	boundless	bower
bouncy	bounty	bowwow

CHOU /tʃaʊ/ — one syllable

chow	_____	_____

O

CHOU /tʃaʊ/—two syllables
chowchow _____ _____
chowder _____ _____

DOU /daʊ/—one syllable
doubt   down   _____
douse   _____

DOU /daʊ/—two syllables
doubter	downfall	downtown
doubtful	downfield	downtrend
doubtless	downgrade	downturn
doughty	downhill	downward
douser	downplay	downwind
douter	downpour	downy
dowel	downrange	_____
downbeat	downright	_____
downcast	downshift	_____
downcourt	downstairs	_____
downdraft	downtime	_____

FOU /faʊ/—one syllable
foul   fount   _____
found   fowl   _____

FOU /faʊ/—two syllables
fouler	foundling	fowler
foulness	foundry	_____
founder	fountain	_____

GOU /gaʊ/—one syllable
gauss   gout   _____
gouge   gown   _____

GOU /gaʊ/—two syllables
gouger	goutweed	_____
gouging	gouty	_____

HOU /haʊ/—one syllable

hound	how	_____
house	howl	_____

HOU /haʊ/—two syllables

hounding	houseguest	howdy
houseboat	household	howler
houseclean	houselights	howling
housecoat	housesit	how-to
housedress	housetop	_____
housefly	housework	_____
houseful	housing	_____

JOU /dʒaʊ/—one syllable

jounce	jowl	_____

KOU /kaʊ/—one syllable

couch	cow	_____
count	cowl	_____

KOU /kaʊ/—two syllables

council	coward	cowlick
counsel	cowbell	cowling
countdown	cowbird	cowshed
counter	cower	kowtow
counting	cowhand	_____
countless	cowherd	_____
county	cowhide	_____

LOU /laʊ/—one syllable

loud	louse	_____
lounge	lout	_____

LOU /laʊ/—two syllables

louder	lounger	loutish
loudly	lounging	lower
loudness	lousy	_____

MOU /maʊ/—one syllable

mound	mouse	_____
mount	mouth	_____

MOU /maʊ/—two syllables

mountain	mousetrap	mouthy
mounted	mousy	_____
mounting	mouthful	_____
mousehole	mouthpiece	_____
mouser	mouthwash	_____

NOU /naʊ/—one syllable

noun	now	_____

POU /paʊ/—one syllable

pouch	pound	pow
pounce	pout	_____

POU /paʊ/—two syllables

pouchy	pounding	power
pouncing	pouter	powwow
poundage	pouting	_____
pounder	powder	_____

ROU /raʊ/—one syllable

round	roust	row
rounds	rout	_____
rouse	route	_____

ROU /raʊ/—two syllables

rounded	roundness	routing
rounder	round-trip	rowdy
roundhouse	roundup	rowel
rounding	roundworm	_____
roundish	rouser	_____
roundlet	rousing	_____
roundly	router	

SOU /saʊ/—one syllable

sough	sow	_____
sound	_____	_____
south	_____	_____

SOU /saʊ/—two syllables

soundboard	soundproof	southward
soundbox	soundtrack	southwest
sounder	southbound	_____
sounding	southeast	_____
soundless	southland	_____
soundly	southmost	_____
soundness	southpaw	_____

SHOU /ʃaʊ/—one syllable

shout	_____	_____

SHOU /ʃaʊ/—two syllables

shouter	shower	_____

TOU /taʊ/—one syllable

tout	town	_____

TOU /taʊ/—two syllables

tousle	townish	_____
towel	townscape	_____
tower	townsfolk	_____
townhouse	township	_____

THOU /ðaʊ/—one syllable

thou	_____	_____

THOU /θaʊ/—two syllables

thousand	thousandth	_____

VOU /vaʊ/—one syllable

vouch	vow	_____

VOU /vaʊ/—two syllables

voucher	vowel	_____
vouchsafe	vower	_____

WOU /waʊ/—one syllable

wound	wow	_____

YOU /jaʊ/—one syllable

yow	_____	_____
yowl	_____	_____

YOU /jaʊ/—two syllables

yowler	_____ _____

ZOU /zaʊ/—one syllable

zounds	_____ _____

OU /aʊ/—final

bough	plow	vow	
bow	pow	wow	
brow	prow	yow	
chow	row	_____	
cow	scow	_____	
how	sow	_____	
now	thou	_____	

OUCH /aʊtʃ/—final

couch	ouch	vouch
crouch	pouch	_____
grouch	slouch	_____

OUD /aʊd/—final

bowed	plowed	_____
cloud	proud	_____
cowed	shroud	_____
crowd	vowed	_____
loud	wowed	_____

OUND /aʊnd/—final

bound	found	mound
browned	frowned	pound
crowned	gowned	round
downed	ground	sound
drowned	hound	wound

OUJ /aʊdʒ/—final

gouge	_____	_____

OUNJ /aʊndʒ/—final

lounge	scrounge	_____

OUL /aʊl/—final

cowl	howl	scowl
foul	jowl	yowl
fowl	owl	_____
growl	prowl	_____

O

OUN /aʊn/—final

brown	down	gown
clown	drown	noun
crown	frown	town

OUS /aʊs/—final

blouse	grouse	mouse
douse	house	spouse
gauss	louse	_____

OUNS /aʊns/—final

bounce	jounce	pounce
flounce	ounce	trounce

OUT /aʊt/—final

bout	drought	grout
clout	flout	lout
doubt	gout	out

pout	shout	stout
rout	snout	tout
route	spout	trout
scout	sprout	_____

OUNT /aʊnt/—final

count	fount	mount

OUTH /aʊθ/—final

mouth	south	_____

OUZ /aʊz/—final

bows	drowse	rouse
browse	house	sows
cows	plows.	vows

OUNDZ /aʊndz/—final

bounds	mounds	sounds
grounds	pounds	zounds
hounds	rounds	_____

U /u/

U /u/ — one syllable

ooh	ooze	oud

U /u/ — two syllables

oodles	oozy	udo
oolong	ouzel	ulu

BU /bu/ — one syllable

boo	boon	boot
boom	boost	booth

BU /bu/ — two syllables

boo-boo	booster	boutique
boohoo	booted	buoy
boomer	bootee	_____
booming	bootlace	_____
boomlet	bootstrap	_____
boondocks	bouffant	_____

CHU /tʃu/ — one syllable

chew	choose	_____

CHU /tʃu/ — two syllables

chewy	choosy	_____
chooser	_____	_____

DU /du/ — one syllable

deuce	dude	dupe
dew	due	_____
do	duke	_____
doom	dune	_____

DU /du/—two syllables

dewdrop	doodle	duty
dewfall	dual	_____
dewy	duet	_____
doer	duo	_____
doings	duple	_____
doodad	duplex	_____

FU /fu/—one syllable

food	fool	_____

FU /fu/—two syllables

foolish	foolscap	_____
foolproof	foozle	_____

GU /gu/—one syllable

goo	goop	_____
goof	goose	_____

GU /gu/—two syllables

goober	goofy	gooseneck
gooey	googol	goulash
goof-off	goopy	_____

HU /hu/—one syllable

hoop	who'd	whoop
hoot	who'll	who's
who	whom	whose

HU /hu/—two syllables

hooey	hooter	who're
hooper	hula	_____
hoopla	whooper	_____
hoopoe	whooping	_____

JU /dʒu/—one syllable

juice	jute	_____

JU /dʒu/—two syllables

jewel	juicer	julep
judo	juicy	junior
jugal	jujube	_____
jugate	jukebox	_____

KU /ku/—one syllable

coo	coot	couth
cool	coup	_____
coop	coupe	_____

KU /ku/—two syllables

coolant	coonskin	cuckoo
cooler	cooter	culottes
cooling	cootie	kudos
coolish	cougar	_____
coonhound	coupon	_____

LU /lu/—one syllable

lieu	loot	lune
loom	lose	lute
loon	loupe	_____
loop	lube	_____
loose	luge	_____

U

LU /lu/—two syllables

looming	loser	lukewarm
loony	losing	lulu
looper	louver	lunar
loophole	luau	lupine
loose-leaf	lucent	_____
loosen	lucid	_____

MU /mu/—one syllable

moo	moon	mousse
mooch	moose	move
mood	moot	

MU /mu/—two syllables

moody	moonlit	movie
moola	moonrise	moving
moonbeam	moonscape	_____
moonfish	moonwalk	_____
moonish	movement	_____
moonlight	mover	_____

NU /nu/—one syllable

gnu	news	noose
knew	newt	nuke
new	noon	_____

NU /nu/—two syllables

newborn	newsroom	nougat
newfound	newsstand	nuisance
newly	newsy	_____
newness	noodle	_____
newsbreak	noonday	_____
newscast	noontide	_____
newsprint	noontime	_____

PU /pu/—one syllable

pooch	pooh	pouf
poof	pool	_____

PU /pu/—two syllables

poodle	poolside	_____

RU /ru/—one syllable

roo	route	runed
rood	roux	ruse
roof	rude	_____
room	rue	_____
roost	rule	_____
root	ruled	_____
rouge	rune	

RU /ru/—two syllables

rhubarb	rootless	ruler
roofer	rootlet	ruling
roofing	rooty	rumor
rooftop	roulade	runic
roomer	roulette	rupee
roomette	router	ruthful
roomful	routine	ruthless
roommate	rubies	_____
roomy	ruble	_____
rooster	ruby	_____
rooted	rueful	_____
rooter	ruin	_____

SU /su/—one syllable

soon	soup	suit
soothe	sue	_____

SU /su/—two syllables

sewage	sucrose	sushi
sewer	suet	suture
sooner	suitcase	_____
soother	suitor	_____
soothing	sumac	_____
souffle	super	_____
soupy	supine	_____

SHU /ʃu/—one syllable

chute	shoes	shoot
shoe	shoo	_____

SHU /ʃu/—two syllables

chutist	shoer	_____
shoebill	shoeshine	_____
shoebrush	shoestring	_____
shoehorn	shoofly	_____
shoelace	shooting	_____

TU /tu/—one syllable

to	toot	two
tomb	tooth	_____
too	tube	_____
tool	tune	_____

TU /tu/—two syllables

toolbox	tuba	tutor
tooling	tubal	tutti
toolroom	tuber	tutu
toolshed	tubing	twofold
toothache	tubule	twosome
toothbrush	tulip	two-step
toothless	tumor	two-tone
toothpaste	tumult	two-way
toothpick	tuna	_____
toothy	tuneful	_____
tootle	tuner	_____
toucan	tune-up	_____
touche	tunic	_____
toupee	tuning	_____

WU /wu/—one syllable

woo	wound	_____

WU /wu/—two syllables

woozy	wounding	_____

WHU /ʍu/—one syllable

whoosh	_____	_____

YU /ju/—one syllable

ewe	you'd	_____
uke	you'll	_____
use	youth	_____
yew	you've	_____
you	yule	_____

YU /ju/—two syllables

ewer	unite	yuletide
U-boat	usage	_____
U-bolt	useful	_____
union	useless	_____
unique	U-turn	_____
unit	youthful	_____

ZU /zu/—one syllable

zoo	_____	_____
zoom	_____	_____

U /u/—final

blew	goo	through
blue	grew	to
boo	knew	too
chew	lieu	true
clue	moo	two
coo	new	who
coup	pooh	woo
crew	roo	yew
dew	rue	you
do	shoe	zoo
drew	shoo	_____
due	shrew	_____
flew	slough	_____
flu	stew	_____
flue	strew	_____
glue	sue	_____
gnu	threw	_____

UB /ub/—final

lube	tube	_____

UCH /utʃ/—final

mooch	smooch	_____
pooch	_____	_____

U

UD /ud/—final

booed	mood	who'd
brood	mooed	wooed
chewed	prude	you'd
cooed	rood	_____
crude	rude	_____
dude	shooed	_____
food	shrewd	_____
glued	sued	_____

ULD /uld/—final

drooled	schooled	_____
fooled	spooled	_____
pooled	tooled	_____
ruled	_____	_____

UMD /umd/—final

bloomed	loomed	_____
boomed	plumed	_____
doomed	roomed	_____
groomed	zoomed	_____

UND /und/—final

pruned	spooned	tuned
runed	swooned	wound

UF /uf/—final

goof	pouf	roof
poof	proof	spoof

UJ /udʒ/—final

scrooge	stooge	_____

UK /uk/—final

duke	nuke	_____
fluke	snook	_____
kook	spook	_____

UL /ul/ —final

cool	school	you'll
drool	spool	yule
fool	stool	_____
pool	tool	_____
rule	who'll	_____

UM /um/ —final

bloom	gloom	tomb
boom	groom	whom
broom	loom	zoom
doom	plume	_____
flume	room	_____

UN /un/ —final

boon	noon	swoon
croon	prune	tune
dune	rune	_____
loon	soon	_____
lune	spoon	_____
moon	strewn	_____

U

UP /up/ —final

coop	loop	troop
coupe	loupe	troupe
croup	scoop	whoop
droop	sloop	_____
dupe	snoop	_____
goop	soup	_____
group	stoop	_____
hoop	swoop	_____

US /us/ —final

deuce	moose	spruce
goose	mousse	truce
juice	noose	_____
loose	sluice	_____

USH /uʃ/—final
whoosh

UT /ut/—final

boot	loot	snoot
brute	lute	suit
chute	moot	toot
coot	newt	
flute	root	
fruit	route	
hoot	scoot	
jute	shoot	

UPT /upt/—final

cooped	scooped	
drooped	snooped	
duped	stooped	
grouped	swooped	
hooped	trooped	

UST /ust/—final

boost	roost	
loosed	spruced	
moussed		

UTH /uð/—final

smooth	soothe	

UTH /uθ/—final

booth	tooth	
couth	truth	
sleuth	youth	

UV /uv/—final

groove	roove	
move	you've	
prove		

UZ /uz/—final

blues	lose	stews
bruise	moos	strews
choose	news	who's
clues	ooze	whose
crews	ruse	zoos
cruise	shoes	_____
dues	shrews	_____
glues	snooze	_____

UZH /uʒ/—final

luge	_____	_____
rouge		

U

YU /ju/

YU /ju/ — one syllable

ewe	you	you've
uke	you'd	yule
use	you'll	_____
yew	youth	_____

YU /ju/ — two syllables

U-boat	unite	you-all
U-bolt	usage	youthful
union	useful	yuletide
unique	useless	_____
unit	U-turn	_____

BYU /bju/ — one syllable

butte	_____	_____

BYU /bju/ — two syllables

beauty	bugler	_____
bugle	butane	_____

DYU /dju/ — one syllable

deuce	dues	_____
dew	duke	_____
dude	dune	_____
due	dupe	_____

DYU /dju/ — two syllables

dewdrop	dual	duple
dewfall	duet	duplex
dewlap	dukedom	duty
dewy	duo	

FYU /fju/ —one syllable

feud	fume	_____
few	fuse	_____
fugue	fuze	_____

FYU /fju/ —two syllables

feudal	fuchsia	**fusion**
fewer	fuel	**futile**
fewest	fugal	**future**
fewness	fumy	_____

GYU /gju/ —two syllables

gewgaw	_____	_____

HYU /hju/ —one syllable

hew	hue	_____
hewn	huge	_____

HYU /hju/ —two syllables

hubris	human	**humor**
hugeness	humane	**humus**
hugeous	humid	_____

KYU /kju/ —one syllable

cube	cue	**cute**

KYU /kju/ —two syllables

coupon	cuing	**kewpie**
cubic	culottes	**kudos**
cubist	cuteness	_____
cubit	cuter	_____
cuboid	cutie	_____
cueist	cutin	_____

MYU /mju/ —one syllable

mew	mule	**mute**
mewl	muse	_____

MYU /mju/—two syllables

mucus	mutant	mutely
mulish	mutate	_____
music	muted	_____

NYU /nju/—one syllable

new	newt	_____
news	nuke	_____

NYU /nju/—two syllables

neutral	newish	newsroom
neutron	newly	newsstand
newborn	newness	newsy
newel	newsbreak	nuance
newer	newscast	nuisance
newest	newsprint	_____
newfound	newsreel	_____

PYU /pju/—one syllable

pew	puce	_____

PYU /pju/—two syllables

pewter	puny	pupil
puma	pupa	putrid

TYU /tju/—one syllable

tube	tune	_____

TYU /tju/—two syllables

tuba	tubule	tuneless
tubeless	tulip	tuner
tubelike	tumor	tune-up
tuber	tumult	tunic
tubing	tuneful	tutor

VYU /vju/—one syllable

view	_____	_____

VYU /vju/—two syllables

viewer	viewpoint	_____
viewing	viewy	_____

WHYU /ʍju/—one syllable

whew	_____	_____

YU /ju/—final

cue	new	yew
dew	pew	you
due	skew	_____
ewe	spew	_____
few	stew	_____
hew	view	_____
mew	whew	_____

YUB /jub/—final

cube	tube	_____

YUD /jud/—final

cued	hewed	spewed
dude	mewed	viewed
feud	skewed	you'd

YUBD /jubd/—final

cubed	tubed	_____

YUJ /judʒ/—final

huge	_____	_____

YUK /juk/—final

cuke	nuke	_____
duke	uke	_____

YUL /jul/—final

mewl	you'll	_____
mule	yule	_____

U

YUM /jum/ —final

fume   spume   _____

YUN /jun/ —final

dune   hewn   tune

YUP /jup/ —final

dupe   _____   _____

YUS /jus/ —final

deuce   puce   use

YUT /jut/ —final

butte   mute   scute

cute   newt   _____

YUTH /juθ/ —final

youth   _____   _____

YUV /juv/ —final

you've   _____   _____

YUZ /juz/ —final

cues   hues   spews

dues   muse   stews

fuse   news   use

fuze   pews   views

hews   skews   _____

U /ʊ/

U /ʊ/ — one syllable
oomph
oops

U /ʊ/ — two syllables
umlaut

BU /bʊ/ — one syllable

book	bush
bull	bushed

BU /bʊ/ — two syllables

boogie	bulgur	bulrush
bookcase	bulldog	bulwark
bookends	bulldoze	bushbuck
booking	bullet	bushel
bookish	bullfight	bushfire
booklet	bullfinch	bushing
booklore	bullfrog	bushwhack
bookmark	bullhead	bushy
bookplate	bullhorn	butcher
bookrack	bullion	
bookrest	bullish	
bookshelf	bullring	
bookstore	bull's-eye	
bookwork	bullsnake	
bookworm	bully	

FU /fʊ/ — one syllable
foot
full

U

173

FU /fʊ/ —two syllables

footage	footlights	footwork
football	footmark	fulcrum
footboard	footnote	fulfill
footbridge	footpath	fullback
footcloth	footprint	fuller
footed	footrest	full-length
footgear	footrope	fullness
foothill	footstep	full-scale
foothold	footstool	full-time
footing	footwear	fulsome

GU /gʊ/ —one syllable

good	goods	_____

GU /gʊ/ —two syllables

good-bye	goodly	goody
goodies	goodness	_____
goodish	goodwill	_____

HU /hʊ/ —one syllable

hood	hoofed	hooked
hoof	hook	hooves

HU /hʊ/ —two syllables

hooded	hoofprint	junta
hoodlum	hookup	_____
hoodwink	hooky	_____

KU /kʊ/ —one syllable

cook	could	_____

KU /kʊ/ —two syllables

cookbook	cooking	couldn't
cooker	cookout	cushion
cookhouse	cookstove	cushy
cookie	cookware	

LU /lʊ/ —one syllable
look

_____ _____

LU /lʊ/ —two syllables
lookout

_____ _____

NU /nʊ/ —one syllable
nook

_____ _____

PU /pʊ/ —one syllable

pull	push	put

PU /pʊ/ —two syllables

pudding	pushball	putoff
pullback	pushcart	put-on
pullet	pushing	put-out
pulley	push-up	put-up
pullout	pushup	_____
pull-up	pushy	_____
pulpit	put-down	_____

RU /rʊ/ —one syllable

rook	room	_____
roof	root	_____

RU /rʊ/ —two syllables

roofer	roomer	rooter
roofing	roomette	rootless
roofless	roommate	rootlet
rooftop	roomy	rooty
rookie	rooted	_____

SU /sʊ/ —one syllable
soot

_____ _____

SU /sʊ/ —two syllables

sooty	superb	_____

U

SHU /ʃʊ/—one syllable

shook	should	_____

SHU /ʃʊ/—two syllables

shouldn't	sugar	sugared

TU /tʊ/—one syllable

took	_____	_____

TU /tʊ/—two syllables

tootsy	_____	_____

WU /wʊ/—one syllable

wolf	woof	_____
wolves	wool	_____
wood	would	_____

WU /wʊ/—two syllables

wolfhound	woodpile	woolpack
wolfish	woodshed	woolsack
woman	woodsy	would-be
woodbine	woodwind	wouldn't
woodblock	woodwork	_____
woodchuck	woodworm	_____
woodcraft	woody	_____
wooded	woofer	_____
wooden	woolen	_____
woodhouse	woolfell	_____
woodland	woolly	_____

WHU /ʍʊ/—one syllable

whoops	_____	_____

UD /ʊd/—final

could	should	would
good	stood	_____
hood	wood	_____

UF /ʊf/—final

hoof	roof	woof

ULF /ʊlf/—final

wolf	_____	_____

UMF /ʊmf/—final

oomph	_____	_____

UK /ʊk/—final

book	look	_____
brook	nook	_____
cook	rook	_____
crook	shook	_____
hook	took	_____

UL /ʊl/—final

bull	pull	_____
full	wool	_____

UM /ʊm/—final

room	_____	_____

UPS /ʊps/—final

oops	_____	_____
whoops	_____	_____

USH /ʊʃ/—final

bush	push	swoosh

UT /ʊt/—final

foot	root	_____
put	soot	_____

UKT /ʊkt/—final

booked	hooked	_____
cooked	looked	_____

USHT /ʊʃt/—final
bushed _____ _____

UDZ /ʊdz/—final
goods   hoods   woods

ULVZ /ʊlvz/—final
wolves _____ _____

UVZ /ʊvz/—final
hooves _____ _____

U /ʌ/

U /ʌ/ — one syllable

of	up	_____
ump	us	_____

U /ʌ/ — two syllables

onion	undone	unlike
other	undress	unlit
oven	undue	unload
udder	unearned	unlock
ugly	unearth	unmade
ulcer	unfair	unmanned
ulna	unfirm	unmarked
ultra	unfished	unmask
umber	unfit	unpack
umpire	unfixed	unpaved
umpteen	unfold	unpeeled
unarmed	unglued	unpile
unasked	unheard	unplug
unbend	unhitch	unrest
unbolt	unhook	unrip
uncap	unjammed	unripe
uncle	unjust	unroll
unclog	unkept	unsafe
uncool	unkind	unsaid
uncouth	unknot	unschooled
uncross	unknown	unseal
uncurl	unlace	unseat
uncut	unlatch	unsew
under	unlearn	unskilled
undid	unleash	unsnap
undo	unless	unstop

U

179

unstuck	unwise	uproar
untie	unwrap	uproot
untied	unzip	upset
unto	upbeat	upside
untold	update	upstairs
untouched	upend	upstate
untrue	up-front	upstream
untruth	upgrade	upstroke
untuned	upgrowth	upsurge
untwined	upheld	upsweep
untwist	uphill	uptight
unused	uphold	uptown
unveil	upkeep	upturn
unvoiced	upland	upward
unwashed	uplift	upwind
unwell	uppish	usher
unwind	upright	utmost
unwired	uprise	utter

BU /bʌ/—one syllable

buck	bulk	bunt
bud	bum	bus
budge	bump	bust
buff	bun	but
bug	bunch	buzz
bulb	bung	_____
bulge	bunk	_____

BU /bʌ/—two syllables

bubble	buckteeth	buffer
bubbly	buckthorn	buffet
bucker	bucktooth	buffy
bucket	buckwheat	buggy
buckeye	budding	bulgur
buckle	buddle	bulky
bucksaw	buddy	bumble
buckskin	budget	bumbling

bummer	bunker	butler
bumper	bunkhouse	butter
bumpy	bunny	button
bunchy	bunter	buzzard
bundle	bunting	buzzer
bungee	busload	_____
bungle	bustle	_____
bunion	busway	_____

CHU /tʃʌ/ —one syllable

chub	chug	chump
chuck	chum	chunk

CHU /tʃʌ/ —two syllables

chubby	chuckle	chunky
chuckhole	chummy	chutney

DU /dʌ/ —one syllable

does	duds	dusk
done	dug	dust
dove	dull	_____
dub	dump	_____
duck	dumps	_____
duct	dun	_____
dud	dunk	

DU /dʌ/ —two syllables

doesn't	duffel	dusky
double	dugout	dustcloth
dovetail	dullish	duster
dozen	dullness	dusting
dubbing	dumbbells	dustpan
duchess	dumpcart	dustproof
duckbill	dumpling	dusty
ducking	dungeon	_____
duckling	dunking	_____
ducky	dunnage	_____

FU /fʌ/—one syllable

fudge	fund	fuss
fun	funk	fuzz

FU /fʌ/—two syllables

fumble	funky	fuzzball
function	funnel	fuzzy
functor	funneled	_____
funfest	funny	_____
fungus	fussy	_____

GU /gʌ/—one syllable

guff	gum	gut
gulch	gums	_____
gulf	gunk	_____
gull	gush	_____
gulp	gust	_____

GU /gʌ/—two syllables

govern	gunky	gutsy
guffaw	gunny	gutter
gullet	guppy	guzzle
gulley	gusher	guzzler
gumball	gushy	_____
gumbo	gusset	_____
gumdrop	gussy	_____
gummy	gusto	_____
gumption	gusty	_____

HU /hʌ/—one syllable

hub	humph	hut
huff	hunch	hutch
hug	hung	_____
hulk	hunk	_____
hull	hunt	_____
hum	hush	_____
hump	husk	_____

HU /hʌ/—two syllables

hovel	huller	hungry
hover	humble	hunky
hubbub	humbler	hunter
hubby	humbug	hunting
hubcap	humdrum	husband
huckster	hummer	husking
huddle	humming	husky
huffy	hundred	hustle
hugger	hunger	_____

JU /dʒʌ/—one syllable

judge	jump	jut
jug	just	_____

JU /dʒʌ/—two syllables

judgeship	jump-off	jungle
judgment	jump-start	junker
juggle	jumpsuit	junket
juggler	jumpy	junkyard
jumble	junco	justice
jumbo	junction	_____
jumper	juncture	_____

KU /kʌ/—one syllable

come	cull	cusp
cub	cult	cut
cud	cup	_____
cuff	cupped	_____

KU /kʌ/—two syllables

color	comfy	coupling
comeback	coming	cousin
comedown	compass	cover
comer	couple	covet
comfit	coupler	cozen
comfort	couplet	cubby

cuddle	cupboard	cutoffs
cuddly	cupcake	cutout
culprit	cupful	cuttage
culture	custard	cutter
cultured	custom	cutting
culvert	cutback	cutup
cumber	cutler	cutwork
cumin	cutlet	kumquat
cunning	cutoff	_____

LU /lʌ/—one syllable

love	lull	lung
luck	lump	lunge
lug	lunch	luxe

LU /lʌ/—two syllables

lovebird	lumbar	lunger
lovely	lumber	luscious
lover	lumpy	luster
loving	luncheon	lustrous
lucky	lunchroom	_____
luggage	lunchtime	_____

MU /mʌ/—one syllable

monk	mug	munch
month	mulch	mush
much	mulct	musk
muck	mull	muss
mud	mum	must
muff	mumps	mutt

MU /mʌ/—two syllables

money	mother	muddler
monger	muckrake	muddy
mongrel	mucky	mudfish
monkey	mudder	mudguard
monthly	muddle	mudhole

muffin	muscle	mussy
muffle	muscled	mustache
muffler	musher	mustang
muggy	mushroom	mustard
mumble	mushy	muster
mummy	muskeg	mustn't
muncher	muskrat	musty
munchkin	musky	mutter
munchy	muslin	mutton
mundane	mussel	muzzle

NU /nʌ/—one syllable

none	null	nut
nub	numb	_____
nudge	nun	_____

NU /nʌ/—two syllables

knuckle	number	nutpick
nothing	numbing	nutshell
nourish	numbly	nutting
nubble	nuptial	nutty
nubbly	nuthatch	nuzzle
nubby	nutmeat	_____
nugget	nutmeg	_____

PU /pʌ/—one syllable

puck	pump	pup
puff	pun	pus
pug	punch	putt
pulp	pung	_____
pulse	punt	_____

PU /pʌ/—two syllables

pomace	pucker	puffbird
pommel	puddle	puffin
public	pudgy	puffy
publish	puffball	pulpy

U

pulsar
pulsate
pumice
pumper
pumping
pumpkin
punchball
punchboard
puncher

punchy
puncture
pungent
punish
punted
punter
puppet
puppy
putter

putty
puzzle
_____
_____
_____
_____
_____
_____
_____

RU /rʌ/—one syllable

rough
rub
ruck
rudd
ruff
rug

rump
run
rung
runt
rush
rusk

rust
rut
wrung
_____
_____
_____

RU /rʌ/—two syllables

rhumba
roughage
rough-cut
roughen
rough-hew
roughhouse
roughish
roughneck
roughshod
rubbing
rubbish
rubble
rubdown
rucksack
ruckus
rudder
ruddy
ruffle

rugged
rumba
rumble
rumbly
rummage
rummy
rumple
rumpus
runback
run-down
runner
run-in
running
runoff
run-through
runty
runway
rupture

rusher
rushing
russet
rustic
rustle
rustler
rustless
rustproof
rusty
rutty
_____
_____
_____
_____
_____
_____

SU /sʌ/—one syllable

some	suds	sung
son	sulk	sunk
sub	sum	sup
such	sump	_____
suck	sun	_____

SU /sʌ/—two syllables

someday	sudden	sunder
somehow	sudsy	sundown
someone	suffer	sundry
someplace	suffix	sunfish
something	suffrage	sunglass
sometime	sulfite	sunglow
sometimes	sulfur	sunlight
someway	sulky	sunny
somewhat	sullen	sunproof
somewhere	sultry	sunray
sonny	summer	sunrise
southern	summit	sunroof
subclass	summon	sunset
subgroup	summons	sunshade
subject	sumpter	sunshine
sublease	sunbath	suntan
subset	sunbathe	sunup
subsoil	sunbeam	sunward
substance	sunblock	supper
subtle	sunbow	supple
suburb	sunburn	suspect
subway	sunburst	suttle
subzone	sun-cure	_____
suction	sundae	_____

SHU /ʃʌ/—one syllable

shove	shun	shut
shuck	shunt	_____
shucks	shush	_____

U

SHU /ʃʌ/—two syllables

shovel	shunter	shuttered
shudder	shutdown	shuttle
shuffle	shuteye	_____
shuffler	shutoff	_____
shuffling	shutout	_____
shunner	shutter	_____

TU /tʌ/—one syllable

ton	tuck	tut
tongue	tuff	tux
touch	tuft	_____
touched	tug	_____
tough	tush	_____
tub	tusk	_____

TU /tʌ/—two syllables

tonnage	toughness	tummy
touchback	tucker	tundra
touchdown	tufted	tunnel
touching	tufty	tussle
touch-tone	tugboat	tussock
touchy	tugging	_____
toughen	tumble	_____
tougher	tumbler	_____
toughish	tumbling	_____

THU /ðʌ/—one syllable

thus	_____	_____

THU /ðʌ/—two syllables

thusly	_____	_____

THU /θʌ/—one syllable

thud	thunk	_____
thumb	_____	_____
thump	_____	_____

THU /θʌ/—two syllables

thumber	thumbtack	thunder
thumbnail	thumper	_____
thumbprint	thumping	_____

VU /vʌ/—two syllables

vulgar	vulpine	vulture

WU /wʌ/—one syllable

once	was	_____
one	won	_____

WU /wʌ/—two syllables

oneness	one-way	wondrous
oneself	wasn't	_____
one-track	wonder	_____

WHU /ʍʌ/—one syllable

what	_____	_____

YU /jʌ/—one syllable

young	yum	_____
yuck	yup	_____

YU /jʌ/—two syllables

younger	yucca	yum-yum
youngest	yucky	_____
youngster	yummy	_____

UB /ʌb/—final

blub	flub	slub
bub	grub	snub
chub	hub	stub
club	nub	sub
cub	rub	tub
drub	scrub	_____
dub	shrub	_____

ULB /ʌlb/ —final
bulb   _____   _____

UCH /ʌtʃ/ —final

clutch	hutch	such
crutch	much	touch

ULCH /ʌltʃ/ —final

gulch	mulch	_____

UNCH /ʌntʃ/ —final

brunch	lunch	_____
bunch	munch	_____
crunch	punch	_____
hunch	scrunch	_____

UD /ʌd/ —final

blood	dud	scud
bud	flood	spud
crud	mud	stud
cud	rudd	thud

UND /ʌnd/ —final

dunned	punned	stunned
fund	shunned	sunned

UF /ʌf/ —final

bluff	muff	stuff
buff	puff	tough
cuff	rough	tuff
fluff	ruff	_____
gruff	scruff	_____
guff	scuff	_____
huff	slough	_____

ULF /ʌlf/ —final
gulf   _____   _____

UG /ʌg/—final

bug	mug	smug
chug	plug	snug
dug	pug	tug
hug	rug	_____
jug	shrug	_____
lug	slug	_____

UJ /ʌdʒ/—final

budge	grudge	sludge
drudge	judge	smudge
fudge	nudge	trudge

ULJ /ʌldʒ/—final

bulge	_____	_____

UNJ /ʌndʒ/—final

lunge	plunge	sponge

UK /ʌk/—final

buck	puck	tuck
chuck	ruck	yuck
cluck	shuck	_____
duck	struck	_____
luck	stuck	_____
muck	suck	_____
pluck	truck	_____

ULK /ʌlk/—final

bulk	skulk	_____
hulk	sulk	_____

USK /ʌsk/—final

brusque	musk	_____
cusk	rusk	_____
dusk	tusk	_____
husk	_____	_____

U

UL /ʌl/—final

cull	hull	null
dull	lull	skull
gull	mull	_____

UM /ʌm/—final

bum	hum	sum
chum	mum	swum
come	numb	thrum
crumb	plum	thumb
drum	plumb	yum
dumb	scrum	_____
from	scum	_____
glum	slum	_____
grum	some	_____
gum	strum	

UN /ʌn/—final

bun	one	stun
done	pun	sun
dun	run	ton
fun	shun	won
none	son	_____
nun	spun	_____

UNG /ʌŋ/—final

bung	rung	swung
clung	slung	tongue
flung	sprung	wrung
hung	strung	young
lung	stung	_____
pung	sung	_____

UNK /ʌŋk/—final

bunk	dunk	gunk
chunk	flunk	hunk
clunk	funk	monk

plunk	slunk	sunk
shrunk	spunk	thunk
skunk	stunk	trunk

UP /ʌp/—final

cup	sup	yup
pup	up	_____

ULP /ʌlp/—final

gulp	pulp	sculp

UMP /ʌmp/—final

bump	grump	slump
chump	hump	stump
clump	jump	sump
crump	lump	thrump
dump	plump	trump
flump	pump	ump
frump	rump	_____

USP /ʌsp/—final

cusp	_____	_____

US /ʌs/—final

bus	plus	truss
fuss	pus	us
muss	thus	_____

UKS /ʌks/—final

bucks	flux	trucks
chucks	luxe	tucks
clucks	plucks	tux
crux	pucks	_____
ducks	shucks	_____

ULS /ʌls/—final

pulse	_____	_____

U

UMPS /ʌmps/ —final
mumps

USH /ʌʃ/ —final

blush	hush	slush
brush	mush	smush
crush	plush	thrush
flush	rush	tush
gush	shush	

UT /ʌt/ —final

but	jut	shut
cut	mutt	smut
glut	nut	strut
gut	putt	tut
hut	rut	

UFT /ʌft/ —final

bluffed	muffed	snuffed
buffed	puffed	stuffed
cuffed	roughed	tuft
fluffed	ruffed	
huffed	scuffed	

UKT /ʌkt/ —final

bucked	ducked	shucked
chucked	duct	trucked
clucked	plucked	tucked

ULT /ʌlt/ —final
cult

ULKT /ʌlkt/ —final

hulked	mulct	sulked

ULPT /ʌlpt/ —final

gulped	pulped	sculpt

UNT /ʌnt/—final

blunt	grunt	shunt
brunt	hunt	stunt
bunt	punt	_____
front	runt	_____

UPT /ʌpt/—final

cupped	supped	_____

UST /ʌst/—final

bussed	gust	thrust
bust	just	trussed
crust	mussed	trust
dust	must	_____
fussed	rust	_____

UNTH /ʌnθ/—final

month	_____	_____

UV /ʌv/—final

dove	love	shove
glove	of	_____

UZ /ʌz/—final

buzz	fuzz	scuzz
does	muzz	was

AIR /ɛər/

AIR /ɛər/ — one syllable

air	ere	heir

AIR /ɛər/ — two syllables

areate	airflow	airwaves
aerie	airlift	airway
airboat	airline	airy
airborne	airmail	arum
air-bound	airplane	heirdom
airbrush	airplay	heiress
air-cool	airport	heirloom
aircraft	airship	heirship
aircrew	airspeed	_____
airdrop	airstrip	_____
airfare	airtight	_____
airfield	airtime	_____

BAIR /bɛər/ — one syllable

bare	bear	_____

BAIR /bɛər/ — two syllables

bareback	bearcat	bearskin
barefaced	bearer	bear's-paw
barefoot	bearing	_____
barely	bearish	_____

CHAIR /tʃɛər/ — one syllable

chair	_____	_____

CHAIR /tʃɛər/ — two syllables

chairlift	chary	_____

DAIR /dɘɛr/—one syllable
dare

DAIR /dɛɘr/—two syllables
dairy	darer	daring
daren't	daresay	

FAIR /fɛɘr/—one syllable
fair	fare

FAIR /fɛɘr/—two syllables
fairer	fairly	fairway
fairgrounds	fairness	farewell

GAIR /gɛɘr/—one syllable
gare

GAIR /gɛɘr/—two syllables
garish

HAIR /hɛɘr/—one syllable
hair	hare

HAIR /hɛɘr/—two syllables
hairbrush	hairpiece	harem
haircloth	hairpin	harewood
haircut	hairstyle	
hairdo	hairy	
hairless	harebell	
hairline	harelike	

KAIR /kɛɘr/—one syllable
cairn	care

KAIR /kɛɘr/—two syllables
carefree	careless	caries
careful	careworn	caring

LAIR /lɛər/ —**one syllable**
lair   laird   _____

LAIR /lɛər/ —**two syllables**
lairdship   _____   _____

MAIR /mɛər/ —**one syllable**
mare   _____   _____

MAIR /mɛər/ —**two syllables**
mare's-nest   mare's-tail   _____

NAIR /nɛər/ —**two syllables**
nares   nary   _____
naris   _____   _____

PAIR /pɛər/ —**one syllable**
pair   pare   _____
paired   pear   _____

PAIR /pɛər/ —**two syllables**
pairing   paring   pear-shaped
parent   pearlike   _____

RAIR /rɛər/ —**one syllable**
rare   _____   _____

V + R

RAIR /rɛər/ —**two syllables**
rarebit   rareness   rareripe
rarely   rarer   raring

SHAIR /ʃɛər/ —**one syllable**
share   shares   _____

SHAIR /ʃɛər/ —**two syllables**
sharecrop   sharing   _____
sharer   _____   _____

TAIR /tɛər/—one syllable

| tare | tear | _____ |

TAIR /tɛər/—two syllables

| teardown | taro | _____ |
| tearing | _____ | _____ |

THAIR /ðɛər/—one syllable

| their | there | they're |
| theirs | there's | _____ |

THAIR /ðɛər/—two syllables

thereat	therein	therewith
thereby	thereof	_____
therefore	thereon	_____
therefrom	thereto	_____

VAIR /vɛər/—two syllables

| varied | vary | _____ |
| varix | _____ | _____ |

WAIR /wɛər/—one syllable

| ware | wear | _____ |
| wares | _____ | _____ |

WAIR /wɛər/—two syllables

| warehouse | wearer | wearproof |
| wareroom | wearing | werewolf |

WHAIR /ʍɛər/—one syllable

| where | where'll | _____ |
| where'd | where's | _____ |

WHAIR /ʍɛər/—two syllables

whereas	wherein	where're
whereby	whereof	whereto
wherefore	whereon	wherewith

AIR /ɛər/ —final

air	heir	swear
bare	lair	tare
bear	mare	tear
blare	pair	their
care	pare	there
chair	pear	they're
dare	prayer	ware
fair	rare	wear
fare	scare	where
flair	share	_____
flare	snare	_____
gare	spare	_____
glare	square	_____
hair	stair	_____
hare	stare	_____

AIRD /ɛərd/—final

aired	glared	spared
bared	haired	squared
blared	laird	stared
cared	paired	where'd
chaired	pared	_____
dared	scared	_____
fared	shared	_____
flared	snared	_____

AIRN /ɛərn/—final

cairn	_____	_____

AIRZ /ɛərz/—final

airs	chairs	glares
bares	dares	hairs
bears	fairs	hares
blares	fares	heirs
cares	flares	lairs

mares	spares	wares
pairs	squares	where's
pares	stairs	_____
pears	stares	_____
prayers	swears	_____
scares	tears	_____
shares	theirs	_____
snares	there's	_____

AR /ær/

AR /ær/ —two syllables

arid	arrant	arrow
aril	arras	_____
aroid	arris	_____

BAR /bær/ —two syllables

baron	barracks	barren
barrack	barrel	barrow

FAR /fær/ —two syllables

farad	farrow	pharynx

GAR /gær/ —two syllables

garret	_____	_____

HAR /hær/ —two syllables

harrass	harrow	_____
harried	harry	_____

KAR /kær/ —two syllables

carat	carom	carry
caret	carrel	karat
carob	carriage	_____
carol	carrot	_____

LAR /lær/ —two syllables

larrup	larry	larynx

MAR /mær/ —two syllables

marriage	marron	marry
married	marrow	_____

V
+
R

NAR /nær/ — two syllables

narrate	narrows	_____
narrow	_____	_____

PAR /pær/ — two syllables

para	parish	parrot
paraph	parrel	parry

TAR /tær/ — two syllables

tariff	_____	_____
tarry	_____	_____

YAR /jær/ — two syllables

yarak	_____	_____
yarrow	_____	_____

AR /ɑr/

AR /ɑr/ — one syllable

arc	are	arm
arch	aren't	armed
arched	ark	art

AR /ɑr/ — two syllables

aardvark	argue	army
aardwolf	argyle	arson
arbor	armband	artful
arcade	armchair	artist
arcane	armful	artless
archduke	armguard	artwork
archer	armhole	arty
archive	armlet	ourself
archpriest	armload	ourselves
archway	armor	_____
arctic	armored	_____
ardent	armpad	_____
ardor	armrest	_____

BAR /bɑr/ — one syllable

bar	barge	barred
barb	bark	_____
barbed	barn	_____
bard	barque	_____

BAR /bɑr/ — two syllables

barbell	barker	barnyard
barber	barky	barter
bardic	barley	_____
bargain	barnstorm	_____

V + R

CHAR /tʃɑr/—one syllable

char	charged	_____
chard	charm	_____
charge	chart	_____

CHAR /tʃɑr/—two syllables

charbroil	charging	charry
charcoal	charmer	charter
charger	charming	_____

DAR /dɑr/—one syllable

dark	darned	_____
darn	dart	_____

DAR /dɑr/—two syllables

darken	darkroom	_____
darker	darling	_____
darkish	darning	_____
darkly	dartboard	_____
darkness	darter	_____

FAR /fɑr/—one syllable

far	farce	farm

FAR /fɑr/—two syllables

far-fetched	farmland	farthest
farmer	farmyard	farthing
farmhouse	far-off	_____
farming	farther	_____

GAR /gɑr/—one syllable

gar	garb	guard

GAR /gɑr/—two syllables

garbage	gargle	garment
garble	garland	garner
garden	garlic	garnet

garnish	guardhouse	_____
garter	guardrail	_____
garvey	guardroom	_____
guarded	_____	_____

HAR /hɑr/—one syllable

hard	harp	_____
hark	harsh	_____
harl	heart	_____
harm	hearth	_____

HAR /hɑr/—two syllables

harbor	hardware	heartache
hardball	hardwood	heartbeat
hardboard	hardy	heartbreak
hard-boil	harken	heartburn
hard-boiled	harmful	heartfelt
hardbound	harmless	hearthstone
hardcore	harness	heartland
harden	harper	heartsick
hardly	harping	heartthrob
hardness	harpist	hearty
hard-shell	harpoon	_____
hardship	harshly	_____
hardtack	harshness	_____
hardtop	harvest	_____

V
+
R

JAR /dʒɑr/—one syllable

jar	_____	_____

JAR /dʒɑr/—two syllables

jarful	jargon	jarless

KAR /kɑr/—one syllable

car	cart	_____
card	carve	_____
carp	_____	_____

KAR /kɑr/—two syllables

caramel	carnage	cartridge
carbon	carpet	cartwheel
carcass	carpool	carver
cardboard	carport	carving
carfare	cartel	karma
cargo	carton	_____
carload	cartoon	_____

LAR /lɑr/—one syllable

larch	large	_____
lard	lark	_____

LAR /lɑr/—two syllables

larder	larger	larkspur
lardy	large-scale	larva
largely	largess	_____
largeness	largo	_____

MAR /mɑr/—one syllable

mar	mark	marsh
march	marl	mart

MAR /mɑr/—two syllables

marble	markup	marshy
marbling	marlin	marten
marcher	marmot	martial
margin	marquee	martin
marker	marquis	martyr
market	marshal	marvel
marking	marshland	_____

NAR /nɑr/—one syllable

gnar	gnarl	gnarled

NAR /nɑr/—two syllables

narwhal	_____	_____

PAR /pɑr/—one syllable

par	parse
parch	part
park	parts

PAR /pɑr/—two syllables

parboil	parlay	parting
parcel	parley	partly
parchment	parlor	partner
pardner	parquet	partook
pardon	parsley	partridge
parfait	parsnip	part-time
parka	parson	partway
parking	partake	party
parkway	parted	
parlance	partial	

SAR /sɑr/—one syllable

sard	sarge

SAR /sɑr/—two syllables

sarcenet	sargo	sergeant
sardine	sari	

SHAR /ʃɑr/—one syllable

shard	shark	sharp

SHAR /ʃɑr/—two syllables

chartreuse	sharp-eyed	sharp-nosed
sharkskin	sharp-freeze	sharp-set
sharp-edged	sharpie	
sharpen	sharply	
sharper	sharpness	

TAR /tɑr/—one syllable

tar	tarp
tarn	tarred

V
+
R

TAR /tɑr/—two syllables

tarboosh	tarpan	tartan
tardo	tarpon	tartar
tardy	tarry	tartness
target	tarsal	tarweed
tarnish	tarsus	_____

VAR /vɑr/—two syllables

varmint	varnish

YAR /jɑr/—one syllable

yard	yare	yarn

YAR /jɑr/—two syllables

yardage	yardstick	yarn-dyed

ZAR /zɑr/—one syllable

czar	_____	_____

ZAR /zɑr/—two syllables

czardom	czarist	_____

AR /ɑr/—final

are	gnar	tar
bar	jar	yare
car	mar	_____
char	par	_____
czar	scar	_____
far	spar	_____
gar	star	_____

ARB /ɑrb/—final

barb	garb	_____

ARCH /ɑrtʃ/—final

arch	march	starch
larch	parch	_____

ARD /ɑrd/—final

bard	guard	shard
barred	hard	sparred
card	jarred	starred
chard	lard	tarred
charred	marred	yard

ARF /ɑrf/—final

scarf	_____	_____

ARJ /ɑrdʒ/—final

barge	large	sparge
charge	sarge	_____

ARK /ɑrk/—final

arc	hark	shark
ark	lark	spark
bark	mark	stark
dark	park	_____

ARL /ɑrl/—final

gnarl	marl	_____
harl	snarl	_____

ARM /ɑrm/—final

arm	farm	_____
charm	harm	_____

ARN /ɑrn/—final

barn	darn	yarn

ARP /ɑrp/—final

carp	sharp	_____
harp	tarp	_____

ARS /ɑrs/—final

farce	sparse	parse

V
+
R

ARSH /ɑrʃ/—final
| harsh | marsh | _____ |

ART /ɑrt/—final
art	dart	part
cart	heart	smart
chart	mart	start

ARTH /ɑrθ/—final
| hearth | _____ | _____ |

ARV /ɑrv/—final
| carve | starve | _____ |

ARZ /ɑrz/—final
bars	gars	spars
cars	jars	stars
chars	mars	tars
czars	scars	_____

AR /ər/

AR /ər/ —two syllables

aright	arouse	arrear
arise	arraign	arrest
arose	arrange	arrive
around	array	awry

BAR /bər/ —two syllables

baroque	barrage	beret
barouche	barrette	_____

GAR /gər/ —two syllables

garage	_____	_____

HAR /hər/ —two syllables

harangue	harrumph	_____
harass	hurrah	_____

JAR /dʒər/ —two syllables

giraffe	_____	_____
jereed	_____	_____

KAR /kər/ —two syllables

carafe	chorale	corrode
careen	corrade	corrupt
career	corral	kaross
caress	correct	_____

MAR /mər/ —two syllables

marine	moraine	morose
maroon	morale	_____
meringue	morass	_____

V
+
R

214 • PAR /pər/—two syllables

PAR /pər/—two syllables

parade	paroled	porrect
paraph	peruke	_____
parole	peruse	_____

SAR /sər/—two syllables

saran	serein	surround
sarod	serene	_____
sarong	sirree	_____

SHAR /ʃər/—two syllables

charade	_____	_____

TAR /tər/—two syllables

terete	terrane	_____
terrain	terrine	_____

VAR /vər/—two syllables

varoom	_____	_____

ER /ir/

ER /ir/ — one syllable
ear   _____   _____

ER /ir/ — two syllables

earache	earmark	earring
eardrum	earmuff	earwax
earful	earphone	eerie
earlobe	earplug	era

BER /bir/ — one syllable

beard	bier	_____

BER /bir/ — two syllables

bearded	beardless	_____

CHER /tʃir/ — one syllable

cheer	cheered	cheers

CHER /tʃir/ — two syllables

cheerer	cheerlead	cheery
cheerful	cheerless	chirrup

DER /dir/ — one syllable

dear	deer	_____

DER /dir/ — two syllables

dearer	dearly	_____
dearest	deerskin	_____

FER /fir/ — one syllable

fear	fierce	_____

V
+
R

215

FER /fir/—two syllables

fearful	feral	fiercer
fearless	fiercely	_____
fearsome	fierceness	_____

GER /gir/—one syllable

gear	_____	_____
gears	_____	_____

GER /gir/—two syllables

gearbox	gearshift	_____
gearing	gearwheel	_____

HER /hir/—one syllable

hear	here	here's

HER /hir/—two syllables

hearer	herein	_____
hearing	hereof	_____
hearsay	hereon	_____
hereat	herewith	_____
hereby	hero	_____

JER /dʒir/—one syllable

jeer	_____	_____

JER /dʒir/—two syllables

jeerer	_____	_____

LER /lir/—one syllable

leer	_____	_____

LER /lir/—two syllables

leery	_____	_____

MER /mir/—one syllable

mere	_____	_____

MER /mir/—two syllables
merely _____ _____

NER /nir/—one syllable
near _____ _____

NER /nir/—two syllables

nearby	nearly	_____
nearer	nearness	_____
nearest	_____	_____
_____		

PER /pir/—one syllable

peer	pier	pierced
peers	pierce	_____

PER /pir/—two syllables

peerage	pierhead	_____
peerless	_____	_____
piercing	_____	_____

RER /rir/—one syllable
rear _____ _____

RER /rir/—two syllables

rearmost	rearward	_____

SER /sir/—one syllable

sear	_____	_____
sere	_____	_____

SER /sir/—two syllables

cerate	serous	_____
series	serum	_____

SHER /ʃir/—one syllable

shear	shears	_____
sheared	sheer	_____

V
+
R

SHER /ʃir/—two syllables

shearer	sheerly	_____
shearing	sheerness	_____

TER /tir/—one syllable

tear	tier	_____

TER /tir/—two syllables

teardrop	tearless	teary
tearful	tearstain	_____

VER /vir/—one syllable

veer	_____	_____

WER /wir/—one syllable

weir	weird	we're

WER /wir/—two syllables

weary	weirdness	weirdo

YER /jir/—one syllable

year	_____	_____

YER /jir/—two syllables

yearbook	yearling	yearly
year-end	yearlong	year-round

ZER /zir/—two syllables

xerarch	xeric	zero

ER /ir/—final

bier	drear	here
blear	ear	jeer
cheer	fear	leer
clear	fleer	mere
dear	gear	near
deer	hear	peer

pier	sneer	we're
rear	spear	weir
sear	sphere	year
sere	steer	_____
shear	tear	_____
sheer	tier	_____
smear	veer	_____

ERD /ird/—final

beard	leered	sneered
bleared	neared	speared
cheered	peered	steered
cleared	reared	tiered
feared	seared	veered
geared	sheared	weird
jeered	smeared	_____

ERZ /irz/—final

cheers	leers	sneers
clears	nears	spears
dears	peers	spheres
ears	piers	steers
fears	rears	tears
gears	sears	tiers
hears	shears	veers
here's	sheers	weirs
jeers	smears	years

V
+
R

ER /ɛr/

ER /ɛr/ — two syllables

era	errand	error
erring	errant	ersatz

BER /bɛr/ — two syllables

berried	beryl	bury
berry	buried	_____

CHER /tʃɛr/ — two syllables

cherish	cherub	_____
cherry	_____	_____

DER /dɛr/ — two syllables

derrick	derris	derry

FER /fɛr/ — two syllables

feral	ferrite	_____
ferrate	ferrous	_____
ferret	ferrule	_____
ferric	ferry	_____

HER /hɛr/ — two syllables

herald	heron	herring

JER /dʒɛr/ — two syllables

gerund	_____	_____

KER /kɛr/ — two syllables

kerry	_____	_____

MER /mɛr/ — two syllables

merit	merry	_____

PER /pɛr/ —two syllables

peril	perish	perron

SER /sɛr/ —two syllables

cerro	serin	serrate
seraph	serine	serry
serif	serow	_____

SHER /ʃɛr/ —two syllables

sheriff	_____	_____

TER /tɛr/ —two syllables

terra	terret	terry
terrace	terror	_____

VER /vɛr/ —two syllables

very	_____	_____

WHER /ʍɛr/ —two syllables

wherry	_____	_____

ZHER /ʒɛr/ —two syllables

gervais	_____	_____

V
+
R

IR /aɪr/

IR /aɪr/ — two syllables

irate   iris   _____

BIR /baɪr/ — two syllables

bireme   _____   _____

HIR /haɪr/ — two syllables

hyrax   _____   _____

JIR /dʒaɪr/ — two syllables

gyral   gyro   gyrose
gyrate   gyron   gyrus

LIR /laɪr/ — two syllables

lyrate   _____

PIR /paɪr/ — two syllables

pirate   pyrite   _____
pyrene   pyrope   _____

SIR /saɪr/ — two syllables

siren   _____   _____

TIR /taɪr/ — two syllables

tirade   tyrant   tyro

THIR /θaɪr/ — two syllables

thyroid   _____   _____

VIR /vaɪr/ — two syllables

viral   virus   _____

ZIR /zaɪr/ — two syllables

ziram   _____   _____

IR /aɪər/

IR /aɪər/ — one syllable

ire

_____ _____

IR /aɪər/ — two syllables

ireful   ireless   _____

BIR /baɪər/ — one syllable

byre

_____ _____

DIR /daɪər/ — one syllable

dire

_____ _____

DIR /daɪər/ — two syllables

direful   direness   _____

direly   direr   _____

FIR /faɪər/ — one syllable

fire   fired   _____

FIR /faɪər/ — two syllables

fiery	fireguard	firewood
fireball	firehouse	fireworks
firebird	firelight	firing
fireboat	fireplace	_____
firebox	fireproof	_____
firebreak	fireside	_____
firebug	firetrap	_____
firefly	fireweed	_____

HIR /haɪər/ — one syllable

hire

_____ _____

V
+
R

HIR /haɪər/—two syllables
hireling   hirer   hiring

JIR /dʒaɪər/—one syllable
gyre   _____   _____

LIR /laɪər/—one syllable
lyre   _____   _____

LIR /laɪər/—two syllables
lyrebird   lyrist   _____

MIR /maɪər/—one syllable
mire   _____   _____

MIR /maɪər/—two syllables
miring   miry   _____

PIR /paɪər/—one syllable
pyre   _____   _____

SIR /saɪər/—one syllable
sire   _____   _____

SHIR /ʃaɪər/—one syllable
shire   _____   _____

TIR /taɪər/—one syllable
tire   tired   _____

TIR /taɪər/—two syllables
tiredness   tiresome   _____
tireless   tiring   _____

WIR /waɪər/—one syllable
wire   _____   _____
wired   _____   _____

WIR /waɪər/—two syllables

wirehaired	wiretap	wiry
wireless	wireworks	_____
wirer	wiring	_____

IR /aɪər/—final

byre	ire	sire
choir	lyre	spire
dire	mire	squire
fire	pyre	tire
gyre	quire	wire
hire	shire	_____

IRD /aɪərd/—final

fired	sired	wired
hired	spired	_____
mired	tired	_____

IRZ /aɪərz/—final

byres	ires	spires
choirs	lyres	squires
fires	quires	tires
gyres	shires	wires
hires	sires	_____

V
+
R

IR /ɪr/

IR /ɪr/—two syllables

erase	erose	irrupt
erect	eruct	_____
erode	erupt	_____

BIR /bɪr/—two syllables

berate	bereft	_____
bereave	_____	_____

DIR /dɪr/—two syllables

derange	derive	_____
deride	direct	_____

LIR /lɪr/—two syllables

lyric	lyrics	_____

MIR /mɪr/—two syllables

mirage	mirror	_____

PIR /pɪr/—two syllables

pyrric	pyrrole	_____

SIR /sɪr/—two syllables

syrinx	syrup	_____

OR /ɔr/, /or/*

OR /ɔr/ — one syllable

oar	or	_____
oared	orb	_____
oars	ore	_____

OR /ɔr/ — two syllables

aura	orbless	ornate
aural	orchard	orphan
oarlock	orchid	ortho
oral	ordain	_____
orange	ordeal	_____
orate	order	_____
orbit	organ	_____

BOR /bɔr/ — one syllable

boar	bored	borscht
board	born	bourn
bore	borne	_____

BOR /bɔr/ — two syllables

boarder	border	boride
boarding	boredom	boring
boardwalk	borer	borrow
boarhound	boresome	_____
borax	boric	_____

CHOR /tʃɔr/ — one syllable

chore	_____	_____

CHOR /tʃɔr/ — two syllables

chortle	_____	_____

*The /ɔr/ and /or/ sounds have been grouped as both pronunciations are accepted for many of these words.

V
+
R

DOR /dɔr/—one syllable

door	dorm	_____

DOR /dɔr/—two syllables

doorbell	doorstop	dormouse
doorknob	doorway	dorsal
doormat	dormant	dory
doorstep	dormer	_____

FOR /fɔr/—one syllable

for	forge	forth
force	fork	four
forced	forked	fourth
ford	form	_____
fore	fort	

FOR /fɔr/—two syllables

forage	forenoon	forte
foray	foresee	fortnight
forbade	foreshock	fortress
forbear	foresight	fortune
forbid	forest	forty
forceful	foretell	forum
forceps	forethought	forward
forearm	forewarn	forwent
forecast	foreword	fourfold
foreclose	forfeit	four-lane
forefront	forger	fourscore
forego	forgo	foursome
foregone	forkful	fourteen
foreground	forklift	fourteenth
forehand	forlorn	fourthly
forehead	formal	four-way
foreign	format	four-wheel
forelimb	former	_____
forelock	forsake	_____
foremost	forsook	_____

GOR /gɔr/—one syllable

gore	gorge	gorse
gored	gorp	gourd

GOR /gɔr/—two syllables

gorgeous	gormand	gory

HOR /hɔr/—one syllable

hoar	horde	horse
hoard	horn	_____
hoarse	horned	_____

HOR /hɔr/—two syllables

hoarding	hormone	horseback
hoarfrost	hornbill	horsehair
hoarsely	hornbook	horseshoe
hoarseness	hornet	horsetail
hoarser	hornpipe	horse-trade
hoary	horrid	_____

KOR /kɔr/—one syllable

chord	cork	corpse
coarse	corked	course
cord	corn	court
cords	corned	_____
core	corps	_____

KOR /kɔr/—two syllables

choral	corded	corkscrew
chorus	cordial	corky
coarsen	cording	cornball
coarsely	cordless	cornbread
coarseness	cordon	corncob
coarser	cordwood	corncrib
coral	corer	corner
cordage	corkboard	cornered
cordate	corker	cornet

V
+
R

cornfield	corsage	courtly
cornflakes	corset	courtroom
cornice	cortege	courtship
cornmeal	cortex	courtyard
cornrow	corvette	_____
cornstalk	courser	_____
cornstarch	coursing	_____
corny	courthouse	_____
corpus	courtier	_____

LOR /lɔr/—one syllable

lord	lore	lorn

LOR /lɔr/—two syllables

laurel	lordly	lorry
loral	lordship	_____

MOR /mɔr/—one syllable

more	morn	mourn
morgue	morse	_____

MOR /mɔr/—two syllables

moral	morpheme	mourner
moray	morrow	mournful
morbid	morsel	mourning
mordant	mortal	_____
mordent	mortar	_____
mores	mortgage	_____
morning	mortise	_____

NOR /nɔr/—one syllable

nor	norm	north

NOR /nɔr/—two syllables

normal	norther	northward
northbound	northern	northwest
northeast	northland	_____

POR /pɔr/—one syllable

porch	pork	pour
pore	port	_____

POR /pɔr/—two syllables

porcine	portage	portrait
poring	portal	portray
porkchop	portend	pourer
porker	portent	_____
porky	porter	_____
porous	porthole	_____
porpoise	portion	_____
porridge	portly	_____

ROR /rɔr/—one syllable

roar	_____	_____

ROR /rɔr/—two syllables

roarer	roaring	_____

SOR /sɔr/—one syllable

soar	source	_____
sore	sword	_____
sort	_____	_____

SOR /sɔr/—two syllables

soarer	sorrel	swordfish
soaring	sorrow	swordplay
sorbet	sorry	_____
sordid	sorted	_____
sorely	sorter	_____
soreness	sortie	_____
sorghum	sorting	_____

SHOR /ʃɔr/—one syllable

shore	short	_____
shorn	_____	_____

V + R

SHOR /ʃɔr/—two syllables

shoreline	shorten	short-range
shoreward	shortening	shortstop
shoring	shorter	short-term
shortage	shortfall	shortwave
shortcake	shorthand	_____
shortchange	shortly	_____
shortcut	shortness	_____

TOR /tɔr/—one syllable

torch	torque	toward
tore	tort	_____
torn	torte	_____

TOR /tɔr/—two syllables

torchlight	torrid	torture
torment	torsade	_____
torpid	torsion	_____
torpor	torso	_____
torrent	tortoise	_____

THOR /θɔr/—one syllable

thorn	_____	_____

THOR /θɔr/—two syllables

thorax	thornbush	thorny

WOR /wɔr/—one syllable

war	warmth	wart
ward	warn	wore
warm	warp	_____

WOR /wɔr/—two syllables

warble	wardrobe	warmish
warbler	wardroom	warmly
warden	wardship	warmness
warder	warmer	warm-up

warning	warren	_____
warpage	warship	_____
warper	warthog	_____
warplane	wartime	_____
warrant	warty	_____

WHOR /ʍɔr/—**one syllable**

wharf	wharves	_____

WHOR /ʍɔr/—**two syllables**

wharfage	_____	_____

YOR /jɔr/—**one syllable**

yore	_____	_____

ZOR /zɔr/—**two syllables**

zori	zoril	_____

OR /ɔr/—**final**

boar	more	sore
bore	nor	spore
chore	oar	store
core	or	swore
corps	ore	tore
door	pore	war
floor	pour	wore
for	roar	yore
fore	score	_____
four	shore	_____
gore	snore	_____
lore	soar	_____

ORB /ɔrb/—**final**

forb	orb	sorb

ORCH /ɔrtʃ/—**final**

porch	scorch	torch

V
+
R

ORD /ɔrd/ —final

board	horde	soared
bored	lord	stored
chord	oared	sword
cord	pored	toward
floored	poured	ward
ford	roared	_____
gored	scored	_____
gourd	shored	_____
hoard	snored	_____

ORF /ɔrf/ —final

corf	dwarf	wharf

ORG /ɔrg/ —final

morgue	_____	_____

ORJ /ɔrdʒ/ —final

forge	gorge	_____

ORK /ɔrk/ —final

cork	pork	torque
fork	stork	_____

ORM /ɔrm/ —final

dorm	norm	swarm
form	storm	warm

ORN /ɔrn/ —final

born	morn	warn
borne	mourn	_____
bourn	scorn	_____
corn	sworn	_____
horn	thorn	_____
lorn	torn	_____

ORP /ɔrp/—final

gorp	warp	_____

ORS /ɔrs/—final

coarse	force	hoarse
course	gorse	horse

ORTS /ɔrts/—final

courts	quartz	sports
forts	shorts	tortes
ports	sorts	warts

ORT /ɔrt/—final

court	quart	sport
fort	short	torte
port	sort	wart

ORST /ɔrst/—final

coursed	forced	_____

ORSHT /ɔrʃt/—final

borscht	_____	_____

ORTH /ɔrθ/—final

forth	fourth	north

V
+
R

ORZ /ɔrz/—final

boars	floors	shores
bores	oars	snores
chores	pores	stores
cores	pours	wars
doors	roars	_____

OUR /aʊr/

OUR /aʊr/—one syllable

hour   our   _____

OUR /aʊr/—two syllables

hourglass   ourself   _____
hourly   ourselves   _____

SOUR /saʊr/—one syllable

sour   _____   _____

SOUR /saʊr/—two syllables

sourball   sourly   sourpuss
sourdough   sourness   _____

OUR /aʊr/—final

flour   our   sour
hour   scour   _____

OURZ /aʊrz/—final

hours   scours   _____
ours   sours   _____

UR /ʊr/

BUR /bʊr/ — one syllable
boor

BUR /bʊr/ — two syllables
boorish   burka   _____
bourgeois   burro   _____

DUR /dʊr/ — one syllable
dour

DUR /dʊr/ — two syllables
dourly   dural   durra
dourness   durance   _____
dura   during   _____

GUR /gʊr/ — two syllables
gourmand   _____   _____
gourmet   _____   _____

JUR /dʒʊr/ — two syllables
jural   jurat   juror
jurant   jurist   jury

LUR /lʊr/ — one syllable
lure

LUR /lʊr/ — two syllables
lurid

MUR /mʊr/ — one syllable
moor

V + R

237

MUR /mʊr/—two syllables

moorage	moorfowl	moorland
moorbird	mooring	_____

NUR /nʊr/—two syllables

neural	_____	_____
neuron	_____	_____

PUR /pʊr/—one syllable

poor	_____	_____

PUR /pʊr/—two syllables

poorer	poorish	poorness
poorhouse	poorly	_____

RUR /rʊr/—two syllables

rural	_____	_____

SHUR /ʃʊr/—one syllable

sure	_____	_____

SHUR /ʃʊr/—two syllables

surefire	surely	surer

TUR /tʊr/—one syllable

tour	_____	_____

TUR /tʊr/—two syllables

touring	tourist	tourney

YUR /jʊr/—one syllable

your	yourn	_____
you're	yours	_____

YUR /jʊr/—two syllables

yourself	_____	_____
yourselves	_____	_____

UR /ʊr/ —final

boor	poor	your
dour	spoor	you're
lure	sure	_____
moor	tour	_____

URD /ʊrd/ —final

lured	_____	_____
moored	_____	_____
toured	_____	_____

URZ /ʊrz/ —final

lures	spoors	yours
moors	tours	_____

V
+
R

YUR /jʊr/

YUR /jʊr/ —one syllable

your	yours	_____
you're	_____	_____

YUR /jʊr/ —two syllables

urine	yourself	yourselves

BYUR /bjʊr/ —two syllables

bureau	burette	burin

DYUR /djʊr/ —two syllables

dural	_____	_____
during	_____	_____

FYUR /fjʊr/ —two syllables

furan	furor	fury

KYUR /kjʊr/ —one syllable

cure	_____	_____

KYUR /kjʊr/ —two syllables

curate	curer	curule
cure-all	curette	kudo
cureless	curie	_____

MYUR /mjʊr/ —one syllable

mure	_____	_____

MYUR /mjʊr/ —two syllables

mural	murine	_____
murex	_____	_____

240

NYUR /njʊr/—two syllables

neural	neutral	_____
neuron	neutron	_____

PYUR /pjʊr/—one syllable

pure	_____	_____

PYUR /pjʊr/—two syllables

pureblood	puree	pureness
purebred	purely	purer

YUR /jʊr/—final

cure	mure	your
dure	pure	you're

YURZ /jʊrz/—final

cures	_____	_____
pures	_____	_____
yours	_____	_____

V
+
R

UR /ɝ/

UR /ɝ/—one syllable

earl	erg	irk
earn	err	urge
earth	herb	urn

UR /ɝ/—two syllables

earldom	earthly	herbal
early	earthquake	herby
earner	earthward	irksome
earnest	earthwork	urban
earning	earthworm	urbane
earthborn	earthy	urchin
earthbound	ermine	urgent
earthen	erring	ursine
earthling	herbage	

BUR /bɝ/—one syllable

berg	birr	burnt
berm	birth	burp
berth	bur	burr
birch	burg	burred
bird	burl	burse
birl	burn	burst

BUR /bɝ/—two syllables

birchen	birdlike	birthday
birdbath	birdseed	birthmark
birdcage	bird's-eye	birthplace
birder	bird's-foot	birthright
birdhouse	bird-watch	birthstone
birdie	birling	borough

242

burble	burlap	burrfish
burbot	burly	burro
burden	burned-out	burrow
burgeon	burner	burry
burger	burning	bursar
burglar	burnish	bursting
burgle	burnout	_____

CHUR /tʃɜ/—one syllable

chert	chirp	churl
chirk	chirr	churn
chirm	church	_____

CHUR /tʃɜ/—two syllables

chervil	chirrup	churner
chirper	churchyard	churning
chirpy	churlish	_____

DUR /dɜ/—one syllable

dearth	dirt	_____
dirge	durst	_____

DUR /dɜ/—two syllables

derma	dirt-cheap	durrie
dirndl	dirty	_____

FUR /fɜ/—one syllable

fern	first	furl
fir	firth	furred
firm	fur	furze

FUR /fɜ/—two syllables

ferment	fervid	first-born
fernlike	fervor	first-class
ferny	firmly	firsthand
fertile	firmness	first-line
fervent	firry	firstly

V
+
R

first-rate	furnish	furtive
first-string	furring	furzy
furbish	furrow	_____
furlong	furry	_____
furlough	further	_____
furnace	furthest	

GUR /gɜ˞/—one syllable

gird	girt	gurge
girl	girth	_____

GUR /gɜ˞/—two syllables

girder	girlhood	gurney
girdle	girlish	_____
girlfriend	gurgle	_____

HUR /hɜ˞/—one syllable

heard	herd	hertz
hearse	herl	hurl
her	herm	hurst
herb	hers	hurt

HUR /hɜ˞/—two syllables

herbage	hurdle	hurry
herbal	hurler	hurtful
herder	hurling	hurtle
herdic	hurly	hurtling
hermit	hurried	_____

JUR /dʒɜ˞/—one syllable

germ	jerk	_____

JUR /dʒɜ˞/—two syllables

gerbil	jerkin	journey
germfree	jerky	_____
germproof	jersey	_____
germy	journal	_____

KUR /kɝ/—one syllable

cur	curl	curt
curb	curled	curve
curch	curse	kerf
curd	curst/cursed	kern

KUR /kɝ/—two syllables

colonel	curlew	curtail
courage	curling	curtain
curbing	curly	curtly
curbside	currant	curtness
curbstone	current	curtsy
curdle	currish	curvy
curdy	curry	kerchief
curfew	cursive	kernel
curler	cursor	_____

LUR /lɝ/—one syllable

learn	lurch	lurk

LUR /lɝ/—two syllables

learned	learning	_____
learner	lurcher	_____

MUR /mɝ/—one syllable

merge	murk	_____
mirth	myrrh	_____

V
+
R

MUR /mɝ/—two syllables

merchant	mermaid	murmur
mercy	mirthful	murrelet
merger	mirthless	murrey
merging	murky	myrtle

NUR /nɝ/—one syllable

knur	knurled	nerve
knurl	nerd	nurse

NUR /nɜ˞/—two syllables

knurling	nourish	nurture
knurly	nursemaid	nurtured
nervous	nursing	_____
nervy	nursling	_____

PUR /pɜ˞/—one syllable

pearl	perm	purl
per	perse	purr
perch	pert	purse
perk	purge	_____

PUR /pɜ˞/—two syllables

pearlfish	permit	purple
pearly	person	purplish
percept	pertly	purpose
percher	pertness	purser
perfect	purchase	purview
perfume	purfle	_____
perjure	purlieu	_____
perjured	purlin	_____
perky	purloin	_____

SUR /sɜ˞/—one syllable

search	serve	surf
serf	sir	surge
serge	surd	_____

SUR /sɜ˞/—two syllables

cermet	serval	surface
certain	servant	surfbird
searcher	server	surfboard
searching	service	surfboat
searchlight	servile	surfeit
serfdom	serving	surffish
sermon	sirloin	surfing
serpent	surcharge	surfperch

surfy	surplice	survey
surgeon	surplus	_____
surly	surrey	_____
surname	surtax	_____

SHUR /ʃɜ˞/ —one syllable

shirk	shirr	shirt

SHUR /ʃɜ˞/ —two syllables

sherbet	shirker	shirttail

TUR /tɜ˞/ —one syllable

term	terse	turn
tern	turf	_____

TUR /tɜ˞/ —two syllables

termite	turgid	turnoff
tersely	turkey	turnout
terseness	turmoil	turnpike
turban	turncoat	turnspit
turbid	turndown	turnstile
turbine	turner	turnup
turbo	turning	turquoise
turbot	turnip	turret
turfy	turnkey	turtle

THUR /θɜ˞/ —one syllable

therm	third	thirst

THUR /θɜ˞/ —two syllables

thermal	thirsty	thirties
thermic	thirteen	thirty
third-class	thirteenth	thorough

VUR /vɜ˞/ —one syllable

verb	verse	verve
verge	versed	_____

V
+
R

VUR /vɜ˞/—two syllables

verbal	vermeil	versus
verdant	vermin	vertex
verdict	vernal	virtue
verging	version	_____

WUR /wɜ˞/—one syllable

were	worked	worst
weren't	world	worth
word	worm	wurst
work	worse	_____

WUR /wɜ˞/—two syllables

wordage	worker	wormhole
wordbook	workhorse	wormy
wording	workhouse	worried
wordless	working	worry
word-lore	workload	worsen
wordplay	workout	worship
wordsmith	workroom	worsted
wordy	workshop	worthless
workbag	work-up	worthwhile
workbench	workweek	worthy
workbook	worldling	_____
workbox	worldly	_____
workday	world-wide	_____

WHUR /ʍɜ˞/—one syllable

whir	whorl	whort
whirl	whorled	_____

WHUR /ʍɜ˞/—two syllables

whirler	whirlwind	whirring
whirlpool	whirly	_____

YUR /jɜ˞/—one syllable

yearn	_____	_____

YUR /jɝ/—two syllables
yearning _____ _____

ZUR /zɝ/—two syllables
zircon _____ _____

UR /ɝ/—final

blur	her	spur
bur	knur	stir
burr	myrrh	were
chirr	per	whir
cur	purr	_____
err	shirr	_____
fir	sir	_____
fur	slur	_____

URB /ɝb/—final

blurb	herb	_____
curb	verb	_____

URCH /ɝtʃ/—final

birch	lurch	smirch
church	perch	_____
curch	search	_____

URD /ɝd/—final

bird	heard	spurred
blurred	herd	stirred
burred	nerd	surd
curd	purred	third
furred	shirred	whirred
gird	slurred	word

URLD /ɝld/—final

curled	knurled	whirled
furled	swirled	whorled
hurled	twirled	world

V + R

URF /ɝf/—final

kerf	surf	_____
serf	turf	_____

URG /ɝg/—final

berg	burg	erg

URJ /ɝdʒ/—final

dirge	scourge	surge
gurge	serge	urge
merge	splurge	verge
purge	spurge	_____

URK /ɝk/—final

chirk	lurk	shirk
clerk	murk	smirk
irk	perk	work
jerk	quirk	_____

URL /ɝl/—final

birl	herl	swirl
burl	hurl	twirl
curl	knurl	whirl
earl	pearl	whorl
furl	purl	_____
girl	skirl	_____

URM /ɝm/—final

berm	herm	term
firm	perm	therm
germ	squirm	worm

URN /ɝn/—final

burn	kern	tern
churn	learn	turn
earn	spurn	urn
fern	stern	yearn

URP /ɝp/—final

burp	slurp	_____
chirp	twerp	_____

URS /ɝs/—final

burse	nurse	terse
curse	perse	verse
hearse	purse	worse

URT /ɝt/—final

blurt	girt	skirt
curt	hurt	spurt
dirt	pert	squirt
flirt	shirt	whort

URST /ɝst/—final

burst	hurst	versed
curst/cursed	nursed	worst
durst	pursed	wurst
first	thirst	_____

URTH /ɝθ/—final

berth	earth	mirth
birth	firth	worth
dearth	girth	_____

V
+
R

URV /ɝv/—final

curve	serve	verve
nerve	swerve	_____

URZ /ɝz/—final

blurs	firs	slurs
burs	furs	purs
burrs	hers	stirs
chirrs	knurs	whirs
curs	purrs	_____
errs	sirs	_____

ER /ɚ/

BER /bɚ/ — **first syllable**

berlin   berserk   burnoose

FER /fɚ/ — **first syllable**

forbid   forget   forgot

forgave   forgive   _____

HER /hɚ/ — **first syllable**

herself   _____   _____

JER /dʒɚ/ — **first syllable**

germane   _____   _____

KER /kɚ/ — **first syllable**

curtail   kerflop   kerplunk

PER /pɚ/ — **first syllable**

percale   perhaps   pertain

perceive   permit   perturb

percent   permute   pervade

perchance   perpend   perverse

perdu   perplex   purloin

perdure   perplexed   purport

perfect   persist   pursue

perform   perspire   pursuit

perfuse   persuade   purvey

SER /sɚ/ — **first syllable**

sirvente   surpass   survey

surmise   surprise   survive

surmount   surveil   _____

VER /vɚ/ — **first syllable**

verbose   virtu   _____

253

ER

ER /ɚr/

AER /eɚ/ —final

brayer	mayor	sayer
flayer	payer	sprayer
grayer	player	strayer
layer	prayer	weigher

ABER /ebɚ/ —final

caber	neighbor	tabor
labor	saber	

AMBER /embɚ/ —final

chamber		

ACHER /etʃɚ/ —final

nature		

ADER /edɚ/ —final

aider	grader	spader
braider	raider	trader
fader	shader	wader

AFER /efɚ/ —final

chafer	safer	wafer

AJER /edʒɚ/ —final

cager	major	sager
gauger	pager	wager

ANJER /endʒɚ/ —final

changer	granger	ranger
danger	manger	stranger

AKER /ekɚ/ —final

acre	faker	raker
baker	maker	shaker
braker	nacre	taker

ALER /elɚ/—final

bailer	nailer	trailer
bailor	paler	wailer
baler	railer	whaler
frailer	sailor	_____
hailer	scaler	_____
haler	staler	_____
jailor	tailer	_____
mailer	tailor	_____

ABLER /eblɚ/—final

abler	fabler	stabler

ADLER /edlɚ/—final

cradler	_____	_____
ladler	_____	_____

APLER /eplɚ/—final

stapler	_____	_____

AMER /emɚ/—final

aimer	framer	namer
blamer	gamer	tamer
claimer	lamer	_____
flamer	maimer	_____

ANER /enɚ/—final

drainer	planer	vainer
feigner	saner	_____
gainer	stainer	_____
grainer	strainer	_____
plainer	trainer	_____

APER /epɚ/—final

caper	paper	taper
draper	scraper	vapor
gaper	shaper	_____

ER

ASER /esɚ/ —final

bracer	lacer	spacer
caser	pacer	tracer
chaser	placer	_____
facer	racer	_____

ASHER /eʃɚ/ —final

glacier	_____	_____

ATER /etɚ/ —final

cater	greater	straighter
crater	hater	tater
dater	later	traitor
freighter	plater	waiter
gaiter	prater	_____
gater	rater	_____
grater	skater	_____

ANTER /entɚ/ —final

fainter	painter	quainter

ASTER /estɚ/ —final

baster	taster	_____
paster	waster	_____

AMSTER /emstɚ/ —final

gamester	_____	_____

ATHER /eðɚ/ —final

bather	_____	_____

AVER /evɚ/ —final

braver	laver	savor
craver	paver	shaver
favor	quaver	waiver
flavor	raver	waver
graver	saver	_____

ALYER /eljɚ/ —final
failure _____ _____

AVYER /evjɚ/ —final
pavior   savior   _____

AZER /ezɚ/ —final

blazer	hazer	raiser
brazer	laser	razor
gazer	mazer	_____
glazer	phaser	_____
grazer	praiser	_____

AZHER /eʒɚ/ —final
brazier   glazier   grazier

ABER /æbɚ/ —final

blabber	drabber	nabber
clabber	gabber	slabber
crabber	grabber	yabber
dabber	jabber	_____

AMBER /æmbɚ/ —final
amber   camber   clamber

ACHER /ætʃɚ/ —final

catcher	patcher	stature
hatcher	scratcher	thatcher
matcher	snatcher	_____

AKCHER /æktʃɚ/ —final
facture   fracture   _____

ANCHER /æntʃɚ/ —final
blancher _____ _____
rancher _____ _____

ER

APCHER /æptʃɚ/—final
rapture _____ _____

ASCHER /æstʃɚ/—final
pasture _____ _____

ADER /ædɚ/—final

adder	gladder	sadder
bladder	ladder	_____
gadder	madder	_____

ANDER /ændɚ/—final

bander	gander	slander
blander	grander	zander
brander	lander	_____
dander	sander	_____

AGER /ægɚ/—final

bagger	gagger	stagger
bragger	lagger	swagger
dagger	nagger	tagger
flagger	sagger	wagger

ANGER /æŋgɚ/—final
anger _____ _____
clangor _____ _____

AJER /ædʒɚ/—final

agger	badger	cadger

AKER /ækɚ/—final

backer	lacquer	tracker
blacker	packer	whacker
clacker	sacker	_____
cracker	slacker	_____
hacker	smacker	_____
knacker	tacker	_____

ASKER /æskɚ/—**final**

asker	masker	_____

ALER /ælɚ/—**final**

pallor	valor	_____

ABLER /æblɚ/—**final**

babbler	dabbler	rabbler
brabbler	gabbler	scrabbler

AMBLER /æmblɚ/—**final**

ambler	rambler	_____
gambler	scrambler	_____

ADLER /ædlɚ/—**final**

paddler	saddler	straddler

ANDLER /ændlɚ/—**final**

chandler	dandler	handler

AFLER /æflɚ/—**final**

baffler	raffler	_____

AGLER /æglɚ/—**final**

haggler	straggler	_____

AKLER /æklɚ/—**final**

cackler	shackler	_____
hackler	tackler	_____

ANGLER /æŋglɚ/—**final**

angler	mangler	wrangler
dangler	tangler	_____
jangler	wangler	_____

AMPLER /æmplɚ/—**final**

ampler	sampler	trampler

ER

ATLER /ætlɚ/—final
battler	rattler	_____
prattler	tattler	_____

ANTLER /æntlɚ/—final
antler	_____	_____

AZLER /æzlɚ/—final
dazzler	_____	_____

AMER /æmɚ/—final
clammer	grammar	slammer
clamor	hammer	stammer
crammer	rammer	yammer
glamour	shammer	_____

ANER /ænɚ/—final
banner	manner	scanner
canner	manor	spanner
fanner	panner	tanner
lanner	planner	_____

ANGER /æŋɚ/—final
banger	clangor	hanger

ANKER /æŋkɚ/—final
anchor	franker	tanker
banker	hanker	thanker
blanker	lanker	_____
canker	rancor	_____
danker	ranker	_____
flanker	swanker	_____

APER /æpɚ/—final
clapper	lapper	rapper
dapper	mapper	sapper
flapper	napper	scrapper

snapper	trapper	zapper
strapper	wrapper	_____
tapper	yapper	_____

AMPER /æmpɚ/—**final**

camper	hamper	tamper
champer	pamper	tramper
clamper	scamper	_____
damper	stamper	_____

ASPER /æspɚ/—**final**

clasper	jasper	_____
grasper	rasper	_____

ASER /æsɚ/—**final**

passer	placer	_____

AKSER /æksɚ/—**final**

laxer	taxer	waxer

ANSER /ænsɚ/—**final**

answer	dancer	prancer
cancer	lancer	_____

ASHER /æʃɚ/—**final**

brasher	hasher	splasher
clasher	masher	thrasher
crasher	rasher	trasher
dasher	smasher	_____

ATER /ætɚ/—**final**

batter	latter	shatter
chatter	matter	smatter
clatter	patter	spatter
fatter	platter	splatter
flatter	ratter	tatter
hatter	scatter	_____

ER

AFTER /æftɚ/—final

after	grafter	wafter
dafter	laughter	_____
drafter	rafter	_____

AKTER /æktɚ/—final

actor	factor	tractor

ANTER /æntɚ/—final

banter	granter	ranter
canter	grantor	scanter
chanter	planter	_____

APTER /æptɚ/—final

apter	chapter	_____
captor	raptor	_____

ASTER /æstɚ/ —final

aster	faster	pastor
blaster	gaster	plaster
caster	laster	raster
castor	master	vaster

AGSTER /ægstɚ/—final

dragster	_____	_____

AKSTER /ækstɚ/—final

quackster	_____	_____

AMSTER /æmstɚ/—final

hamster	_____	_____

ANGSTER /æŋstɚ/—final

gangster	_____	_____

ANKSTER /æŋkstɚ/—final

prankster	_____	_____

ATHER /æðɚ/—final

blather	lather	slather
gather	rather	_____

ANTHER /ænθɚ/—final

anther	panther	_____

ALVER /ælvɚ/—final

salver	salvor	_____

AZER /æzɚ/—final

lazar	jazzer	_____

AZHER /æʒɚ/—final

azure	_____	_____

AFCHER /ɑftʃɚ/—final

wafture	_____	_____

AGER /ɑgɚ/—final

agar	_____	_____

AMER /ɑmɚ/—final

calmer	palmar	_____

ALMER /ɑlmɚ/—final

palmar	_____	_____

ATER /ɑtɚ/—final

quatre	_____	_____

AFTER /ɑftɚ/—final

wafter	_____	_____

ATHER /ɑðɚ/—final

father	_____	_____

ER

AVER /ɑvɚ/—final
suaver

EER /iɚ/—final

fleer	seer	
freer	skier	

ECHER /itʃɚ/—final

beacher	feature	reacher
bleacher	leacher	screecher
creature	preacher	teacher

EDER /idɚ/—final

beader	kneader	speeder
bleeder	leader	weeder
breeder	needer	
cedar	pleader	
feeder	reader	
heeder	seeder	

ELDER /ildɚ/—final

fielder	wielder	
shielder	yielder	

EFER /ifɚ/—final
briefer

EGER /igɚ/—final

eager	meager	
leaguer		

EKER /ikɚ/—final

beaker	shrieker	weaker
bleaker	sleeker	wreaker
leaker	sneaker	
meeker	speaker	
seeker	squeaker	

ELER /ilɚ/—final

dealer	peeler	**wheeler**
feeler	reeler	_____
healer	sealer	_____
heeler	spieler	_____
kneeler	squealer	_____

EBLER /iblɚ/—final

feebler	_____	_____

EDLER /idlɚ/—final

needler	_____	_____
wheedler	_____	_____

EMER /imɚ/—final

creamer	screamer	**teamer**
dreamer	seemer	_____
femur	steamer	_____
schemer	streamer	_____

ENER /inɚ/—final

cleaner	keener	**preener**
gleaner	leaner	_____
greener	meaner	_____

EPER /ipɚ/—final

beeper	leaper	**weeper**
cheaper	peeper	_____
cheeper	reaper	_____
creeper	sleeper	_____
deeper	steeper	_____
keeper	sweeper	_____

ER

ESER /isɚ/—final

creaser	leaser	_____
fleecer	piecer	_____
greaser	_____	_____

ETER /itɚ/—final

beater	liter	tweeter
cheater	meter	_____
eater	neater	_____
fleeter	sweeter	_____
greeter	teeter	_____
heater	treater	_____

ESTER /istɚ/—final

feaster	_____	_____

EDSTER /idstɚ/—final

speedster	_____	_____

EMSTER /imstɚ/—final

teamster	_____	_____

ETHER /iðɚ/—final

breather	neither	teether
either	sheather	_____

ETHER /iθɚ/—final

ether	_____	_____

EVER /ivɚ/—final

beaver	griever	lever
cleaver	heaver	weaver
fever	leaver	weever

ENYER /injɚ/—final

senior	_____	_____

EZER /izɚ/—final

easer	seizer	tweezer
freezer	sneezer	wheezer
geezer	squeezer	_____
pleaser	teaser	_____

EZHER /iʒɚ/—final
leisure   seizure   _____

EMBER /ɛmbɚ/—final
ember   member   _____

ECHER /ɛtʃɚ/—final
| etcher | fletcher | stretcher |
| fetcher | sketcher | _____ |

EKCHER /ɛktʃɚ/—final
lecture   _____   _____

ELCHER /ɛltʃɚ/—final
squelcher   _____   _____

ENCHER /ɛntʃɚ/—final
bencher	drencher	venture
blencher	quencher	wrencher
denture	trencher	_____

ESCHER /ɛstʃɚ/—final
| gesture | _____ | _____ |
| vesture | _____ | _____ |

EKSCHER /ɛkstʃɚ/—final
texture   _____   _____

EDER /ɛdɚ/—final
cheddar	shedder	threader
deader	shredder	treader
header	sledder	_____
redder	spreader	_____

ER

ELDER /ɛldɚ/—final
| elder | _____ | _____ |
| welder | _____ | _____ |

ENDER /ɛndɚ/ —final

blender	mender	spender
fender	render	splendor
gender	sender	tender
lender	slender	vendor

EFER /ɛfɚ/ —final

deafer	heifer	zephyr

EGER /ɛgɚ/ —final

beggar	egger	_____

EJER /ɛdʒɚ/ —final

dredger	hedger	pledger
edger	ledger	_____

EKER /ɛkɚ/ —final

checker	decker	wrecker

ELER /ɛlɚ/ —final

cellar	sheller	sweller
dweller	smeller	teller
queller	speller	_____
seller	stellar	_____

EDLER /ɛdlɚ/ —final

meddler	peddler	treadler

EKLER /ɛklɚ/ —final

heckler	_____	_____

EMBLER /ɛmblɚ/ —final

trembler	_____	_____

ESLER /ɛslɚ/ —final

wrestler	_____	_____
nestler		

ETLER /ɛtlɚ/ **—final**
nettler
settler

EMER /ɛmɚ/ **—final**
hemmer   stemmer   tremor

ENER /ɛnɚ/ **—final**
penner   tenor

EPER /ɛpɚ/ **—final**
leper   pepper   stepper

ELPER /ɛlpɚ/ **—final**
helper   yelper

EMPER /ɛmpɚ/ **—final**
temper

ESPER /ɛspɚ/ **—final**
vesper

ESER /ɛsɚ/ **—final**
dresser   lesser
guesser   stressor

EKSER /ɛksɚ/ **—final**
flexor
vexer

ER

ENSER /ɛnsɚ/ **—final**
censor   fencer   tensor
denser   tenser

ESHER /ɛʃɚ/ **—final**
fresher   pressure   thresher

EKSHER /ɛkʃɚ/ —final
flexure

ELSHER /ɛlʃɚ/ —final
welsher

ENSHER /ɛnʃɚ/ —final
censure

ETER /ɛtɚ/ —final

better	getter	whetter
bettor	letter	
debtor	setter	
fetter	sweater	
fretter	wetter	

EKTER /ɛktɚ/ —final

lector	sector	
nectar	specter	
rector	vector	

ELTER /ɛltɚ/ —final

melter	svelter	
pelter	swelter	
shelter	welter	
smelter		

ENTER /ɛntɚ/ —final

center	renter	
enter	tenter	
mentor		

EPTER /ɛptɚ/ —final
scepter

EMPTER /ɛmptɚ/ —final
tempter

ESTER /ɛstɚ/ — final

ester	pester	wester
fester	quester	wrester
jester	rester	_____
nester	tester	_____

ETHER /ɛðɚ/ — final

feather	nether	whether
heather	tether	_____
leather	weather	_____

EVER /ɛvɚ/ — final

clever	lever	sever
ever	never	_____

ELVER /ɛlvɚ/ — final

delver	elver	shelver

ENZER /ɛnzɚ/ — final

cleanser	_____	_____

EZHER /ɛʒɚ/ — final

measure	pleasure	treasure

IER /aɪɚ/ — final

brier	liar	tier
buyer	nigher	trier
crier	plier	vier
drier	prier	wrier
dryer	prior	_____
flier	shier	_____
friar	sigher	_____
fryer	slier	_____
higher	spryer	_____

IBER /aɪbɚ/ — final

briber	fiber	scriber

ER

IDER /aɪdɚ/ —final

chider	hider	strider
cider	rider	stridor
eider	slider	wider
glider	snider	_____
guider	spider	_____

ILDER /aɪldɚ/ —final

milder	wilder	_____

INDER /aɪndɚ/ —final

binder	finder	kinder
blinder	grinder	winder

IFER /aɪfɚ/ —final

cipher	fifer	lifer

IGER /aɪgɚ/ —final

tiger	_____	_____

IKER /aɪkɚ/ —final

biker	piker	striker
hiker	spiker	_____

ILER /aɪlɚ/ —final

dialer	pilar	tiler
filer	smiler	_____
miler	styler	_____

IDLER /aɪdlɚ/ —final

bridler	idler	_____

IFLER /aɪflɚ/ —final

rifler	stifler	trifler

IKLER /aɪklɚ/ —final

cycler	_____	_____

IMER /aɪmɚ/—final

chimer	mimer	rhymer
climber	primer	timer

INER /aɪnɚ/—final

diner	miner	signer
finer	minor	whiner
liner	shiner	_____

IPER /aɪpɚ/—final

diaper	sniper	_____
griper	striper	_____
piper	viper	_____
riper	wiper	_____

ISER /aɪsɚ/—final

dicer	pricer	slicer
nicer	ricer	splicer

ITER /aɪtɚ/—final

biter	righter	writer
brighter	sighter	_____
fighter	slighter	_____
kiter	smiter	_____
lighter	tighter	_____
miter	whiter	_____

ISTER /aɪstɚ/—final

heister	_____	_____

ER

ITHER /aɪðɚ/—final

either	neither	_____
lither	tither	_____

IVER /aɪvɚ/—final

diver	fiver	thriver
driver	striver	_____

IZER /aɪzɚ/—final

geyser	riser	wiser
kaiser	sizer	_____
miser	visor	_____

IBER /ɪbɚ/—final

cribber	gibber	jibber
fibber	glibber	_____

IMBER /ɪmbɚ/—final

limber	timber	_____

ICHER /ɪtʃɚ/—final

ditcher	richer	switcher
hitcher	snitcher	twitcher
pitcher	stitcher	_____

IKCHER /ɪktʃɚ/—final

picture	_____	_____
stricture	_____	_____

IKSCHER /ɪkstʃɚ/—final

fixture	mixture

INCHER /ɪntʃɚ/—final

clincher	pincher	_____
flincher	wincher	_____

INKCHER /ɪŋktʃɚ/—final

tincture	_____	_____

IDER /ɪdɚ/—final

bidder	kidder	_____
gridder	skidder	_____

ILDER /ɪldɚ/—final

builder	gilder	guilder

INDER /ɪndɚ/ —**final**

cinder	tinder	_____
hinder	_____	_____

IFER /ɪfɚ/ —**final**

differ	_____	_____
stiffer	_____	_____

ILFER /ɪlfɚ/ —**final**

pilfer	_____	_____

IGER /ɪgɚ/ —**final**

bigger	rigor	_____
chigger	snigger	_____
digger	trigger	_____
jigger	vigor	_____

INJER /ɪndʒɚ/ —**final**

cringer	injure	_____
ginger	singer	_____

IKER /ɪkɚ/ —**final**

bicker	pricker	ticker
clicker	quicker	vicar
dicker	sicker	whicker
flicker	slicker	wicker
kicker	snicker	_____
nicker	sticker	_____
picker	thicker	_____

ILKER /ɪlkɚ/ —**final**

bilker	_____	_____
milker	_____	_____

ISKER /ɪskɚ/ —**final**

brisker	risker	_____
frisker	whisker	_____

ER

ILER /ɪlɚ/—final

chiller	miller	stiller
driller	pillar	thriller
filler	quiller	tiller
griller	shriller	_____

IBLER /ɪblɚ/—final

dibbler	fribbler	quibbler
dribbler	nibbler	scribbler

IMBLER /ɪmblɚ/—final

nimbler	_____	_____

IDLER /ɪdlɚ/—final

fiddler	piddler	twiddler

IFLER /ɪflɚ/—final

sniffler	riffler	whiffler

IGLER /ɪglɚ/—final

giggler	sniggler	_____
higgler	wiggler	_____

IKLER /ɪklɚ/—final

stickler	_____	_____
tickler	_____	_____

INGLER /ɪŋglɚ/—final

jingler	shingler	_____
mingler	tingler	_____

INKLER /ɪŋklɚ/—final

sprinkler	twinkler	_____

IPLER /ɪplɚ/—final

crippler	_____	_____
rippler	_____	_____

IMPLER /ɪmplɚ/ **—final**
simpler _____ _____

ISLER /ɪslɚ/ **—final**
whistler _____ _____

ITLER /ɪtlɚ/ **—final**
brittler   littler   whittler

IZLER /ɪzlɚ/ **—final**
chiseler   grizzler   sizzler

IMER /ɪmɚ/ **—final**
brimmer	primer	swimmer
dimmer	shimmer	trimmer
glimmer	simmer	_____
grimmer	skimmer	_____
krimmer	slimmer	_____

INER /ɪnɚ/ **—final**
dinner	skinner	_____
grinner	spinner	_____
inner	thinner	_____
pinner	tinner	_____
sinner	winner	_____

INGER /ɪŋɚ/ **—final**
bringer	springer	zinger
clinger	stinger	_____
flinger	stringer	_____
ringer	swinger	_____
singer	winger	_____
slinger	wringer	_____

ER

INGGER /ɪŋgɚ/ **—final**
finger _____ _____
linger _____ _____

INKER /ɪŋkɚ/—final

blinker	prinker	winker
clinker	shrinker	_____
inker	sinker	_____
linker	stinker	_____
pinker	thinker	_____
plinker	tinker	_____

IPER /ɪpɚ/—final

chipper	gypper	slipper
clipper	kipper	snipper
dipper	lipper	tipper
dripper	shipper	tripper
flipper	sipper	zipper
gripper	skipper	

IMPER /ɪmpɚ/—final

crimper	shrimper	whimper
limper	simper	_____

ISPER /ɪspɚ/—final

crisper	lisper	whisper

ISER /ɪsɚ/—final

hisser	_____	_____
kisser	_____	_____

IKSER /ɪksɚ/—final

fixer	_____	_____
mixer	_____	_____

INSER /ɪnsɚ/—final

mincer	pincer	wincer

ISHER /ɪʃɚ/—final

fisher	swisher	_____
fissure	wisher	_____

ITER /ɪtɚ/—final

bitter	hitter	skitter
critter	jitter	spitter
fitter	knitter	splitter
flitter	litter	titter
fritter	pitter	twitter
glitter	quitter	_____
gritter	sitter	_____

IFTER /ɪftɚ/—final

drifter	shifter	swifter
lifter	sifter	_____

IKTER /ɪktɚ/—final

stricter	victor	_____

ILTER /ɪltɚ/—final

filter	kilter	quilter
jilter	philter	tilter

INTER /ɪntɚ/—final

hinter	splinter	stinter
minter	sprinter	tinter
printer	squinter	winter

IPTER /ɪptɚ/—final

scripter	_____	_____

IPSTER /ɪpstɚ/—final

quipster	_____	_____

ER

ISTER /ɪstɚ/—final

blister	lister	sister
grister	mister	twister

IKSTER /ɪkstɚ/—final

trickster	_____	_____

INSTER /ɪnstɚ/—final
spinster

ITHER /ɪðɚ/—final

blither	slither	wither
dither	thither	
hither	whither	

ITHER /ɪθɚ/—final
zither

IVER /ɪvɚ/—final

giver	quiver	shiver
liver	river	sliver

ILVER /ɪlvɚ/—final
silver

IGYER /ɪgjɚ/—final
figure

IZER /ɪzɚ/—final

fizzer	quizzer	whizzer
frizzer	scissor	

OER /oɚ/—final

blower	lower	sower
crower	mower	thrower
goer	rower	tower
grower	sewer	
hoer	slower	

OBER /obɚ/—final

prober	rober	sober

OCHER /otʃɚ/—final

coacher	poacher	

ODER /odɚ/—final

coder	odor	_____
loader	_____	_____

OLDER /oldɚ/—final

bolder	holder	scolder
boulder	molder	shoulder
colder	older	smolder
folder	polder	_____

OFER /ofɚ/—final

chauffeur	gopher	_____
gofer	loafer	_____

OGER /ogɚ/—final

ogre	_____	_____

OKER /okɚ/—final

broker	joker	soaker
choker	ocher	stoker
croaker	poker	_____

OLER /olɚ/—final

bowler	polar	stroller
coaler	poller	toller
droller	roller	troller
molar	solar	volar

OBLER /oblɚ/—final

nobler	_____	_____

OLJER /oldʒɚ/—final

soldier	_____	_____

OMER /omɚ/—final

comber	roamer	_____
homer	vomer	_____

ER

ONER /onɚ/ —final

boner	droner	loner
cloner	groaner	owner
donor	loaner	toner

OPER /opɚ/ —final

hoper	roper	_____
moper	sloper	_____

OSER /osɚ/ —final

closer	grocer	grosser

OKSER /oksɚ/ —final

coaxer	hoaxer	_____

OSHER /oʃɚ/ —final

kosher	_____	_____

OTER /otɚ/ —final

bloater	gloater	toter
boater	motor	voter
doter	quoter	_____
floater	rotor	_____

OLTER /oltɚ/ —final

bolter	jolter	_____
colter	molter	_____

OSTER /ostɚ/ —final

boaster	poster	toaster
coaster	roaster	_____

OKSTER /okstɚ/ —final

jokester	_____	_____

OLSTER /olstɚ/ —final

bolster	pollster	_____

OLDSTER /oldstɚ/—final
oldster

OVER /ovɚ/—final

clover	over	rover
drover	plover	trover

OZER /ozɚ/—final

closer	dozer	poser

OZHER /oʒɚ/—final

closure	hosier	osier

OBER /ɒbɚ/—final

bobber	jobber	robber
clobber	lobber	slobber
dobber	mobber	sobber

OMBER /ɒmbɚ/—final
somber

OCHER /ɒtʃɚ/—final
botcher
watcher

ODER /ɒdɚ/—final

dodder	odder	solder
fodder	plodder	squadder
nodder	prodder	wadder

ONDER /ɒndɚ/—final

blonder	ponder	yonder
bonder	squander	
fonder	wander	

OFER /ɒfɚ/—final

doffer	goffer	proffer

ER

OLFER /ɒlfɚ/ —final
golfer   _____   _____

OGER /ɒgɚ/ —final

fogger	logger	
jogger	slogger	

OJER /ɒdʒɚ/ —final

codger	lodger	
dodger	roger	

ONJER /ɒndʒɚ/ —final
conjure   _____   _____

OKER /ɒkɚ/ —final

blocker	locker	stocker
clocker	mocker	
docker	rocker	
hocker	shocker	
knocker	soccer	

OLER /ɒlɚ/ —final

collar	holler	scholar
dollar	loller	squalor

OBLER /ɒblɚ/ —final

cobbler	hobbler	wobbler
gobbler	squabbler	

ODLER /ɒdlɚ/ —final

coddler	toddler	waddler

OGLER /ɒglɚ/ —final

boggler	toggler	joggler

OPLER /ɒplɚ/ —final
poplar   _____   _____

OSLER /ɒslɚ/ —**final**
jostler

ONER /ɒnɚ/ —**final**
honor

ONGGER /ɒŋgɚ/ —**final**

conger	monger	
longer	stronger	

ONKER /ɒŋkɚ/ —**final**

conker	conquer	honker

OPER /ɒpɚ/ —**final**

bopper	flopper	stopper
chopper	hopper	swapper
copper	lopper	topper
cropper	proper	whopper
dropper	shopper	

OMPER /ɒmpɚ/ —**final**

romper	stomper	swamper

OSER /ɒsɚ/ —**final**

dosser	glosser	tosser

OKSER /ɒksɚ/ —**final**
boxer

ONSER /ɒnsɚ/ —**final**
sponsor

OSHER /ɒʃɚ/ —**final**

josher	squasher	washer

ONSHER /ɒnʃɚ/ —**final**
tonsure

OTER /ɒtɚ/ —final

blotter	knotter	spotter
cotter	otter	squatter
dotter	plotter	swatter
hotter	potter	trotter
jotter	rotter	_____

OKTER /ɒktɚ/ —final

doctor	proctor	_____

OMPTER /ɒmptɚ/ —final

prompter	_____	_____

OPTER /ɒptɚ/ —final

copter	_____	_____

OSTER /ɒstɚ/ —final

foster	roster	_____

OBSTER /ɒbstɚ/ —final

lobster	mobster	_____

ONSTER /ɒnstɚ/ —final

monster	_____	_____

ONGSTER /ɒŋstɚ/ —final

songster	_____	_____

OTHER /ɒðɚ/ —final

bother	pother	_____

OER /ɔɚ/ —final

clawer	gnawer	rawer
drawer	pawer	sawer

OBER /ɔbɚ/ —final

dauber	_____	_____

ONCHER /ɔntʃɚ/—final
launcher
stauncher

ODER /ɔdɚ/—final
broader
lauder

OLDER /ɔldɚ/—final
alder
balder

ONDER /ɔndɚ/—final
launder   maunder

OFER /ɔfɚ/—final
coffer	doffer	scoffer
cougher	offer	

OGER /ɔgɚ/—final
auger	dogger	logger
augur	hogger	

OKER /ɔkɚ/—final
balker	hawker	talker
calker	squawker	walker
caulker	stalker	

OLER /ɔlɚ/—final
bawler	faller	sprawler
brawler	hauler	squaller
caller	mauler	taller
crawler	scrawler	trawler
drawler	smaller	

ODLER /ɔdlɚ/—final
dawdler

ER

ONER /ɔnɚ/—final

awner	goner	spawner
fawner	pawner	yawner

ONGER /ɔŋɚ/—final

wronger

ONGGER /ɔŋgɚ/—final

longer

stronger

OPER /ɔpɚ/—final

pauper

yawper

OSER /ɔsɚ/—final

crosser	glosser	saucer
flosser	rosser	tosser

OTER /ɔtɚ/—final

daughter	tauter	
slaughter	water	

OFTER /ɔftɚ/—final

softer

OLTER /ɔltɚ/—final

altar	halter	vaulter
alter	palter	
falter	salter	

ONTER /ɔntɚ/—final

flaunter	haunter	vaunter
gaunter	taunter	

OTHER /ɔθɚ/—final

author

OYER /ɔjɚ/ **—final**

lawyer	sawyer	_____

OZER /ɔzɚ/ **—final**

causer	hawser	pauser

OIER /ɔɪɚ/ **—final**

coyer	lawyer	_____
foyer	toyer	_____

OISCHER /ɔɪstʃɚ/ **—final**

moisture	_____	_____

OIDER /ɔɪdɚ/ **—final**

voider	_____	_____

OINDER /ɔɪndɚ/ **—final**

joinder	_____	_____

OILER /ɔɪlɚ/ **—final**

boiler	moiler	toiler
broiler	oiler	_____
coiler	spoiler	_____

OINER /ɔɪnɚ/ **—final**

coiner	joiner	_____

OISER /ɔɪsɚ/ **—final**

choicer	_____	_____
voicer	_____	_____

OITER /ɔɪtɚ/ **—final**

goiter	_____	_____
loiter	_____	_____

OINTER /ɔɪntɚ/ **—final**

jointer	pointer	_____

ER

OISTER /ɔɪstɚ/ —final

cloister	moister	roister
hoister	oyster	_____

OILYER /ɔɪljɚ/ —final

soilure	_____	_____

OUER /aʊɚ/ —final

bower	flower	shower
cower	plower	tower
dower	power	vower

OUCHER /aʊtʃɚ/ —final

croucher	sloucher	voucher

OUDER /aʊdɚ/ —final

chowder	powder	_____
louder	prouder	_____

OUNDER /aʊndɚ/ —final

flounder	hounder	sounder
founder	pounder	_____
grounder	rounder	_____

OUGER /aʊdʒɚ/ —final

gouger	_____	_____

OUNJER /aʊndʒɚ/ —final

lounger	scrounger	_____

OULER /aʊlɚ/ —final

fouler	howler	yowler
fowler	prowler	_____
growler	scowler	_____

OUSER /aʊsɚ/ —final

grouser	douser

OUNSER /aʊnsɚ/—**final**

bouncer	pouncer	_____
ouncer	trouncer	_____

OUTER /aʊtɚ/—**final**

doubter	pouter	spouter
flouter	router	stouter
grouter	scouter	touter
outer	shouter	_____

OUNTER /aʊntɚ/—**final**

counter	_____	_____

OUSTER /aʊstɚ/—**final**

ouster	_____	_____

OUTHER /aʊðɚ/—**final**

souther	_____	_____

OUZER /aʊzɚ/—**final**

browser	mouser	schnauzer
dowser	rouser	trouser

UER /uɚ/—**final**

bluer	newer	strewer
chewer	ruer	suer
doer	sewer	truer
ewer	shoer	who're
gluer	shooer	wooer

UBER /ubɚ/—**final**

goober	_____	_____
tuber	_____	_____

UCHER /utʃɚ/—**final**

moocher	_____	_____
suture	_____	_____

ER

UDER /udɚ/—final

brooder	ruder	_____
cruder	shrewder	_____

UFER /ufɚ/—final

hoofer	roofer	_____

UGER /ugɚ/—final

cougar	_____	_____

UJER /udʒɚ/—final

smoodger	_____	_____

UKER /ukɚ/—final

blucher	lucre	_____

ULER /ulɚ/—final

cooler	ruler	tooler

UMER /umɚ/—final

bloomer	groomer	rumor
boomer	roomer	tumor

UNER /unɚ/—final

crooner	pruner	sooner
lunar	schooner	tuner

UPER /upɚ/—final

blooper	looper	trooper
cooper	scooper	trouper
duper	snooper	whooper
grouper	stupor	_____
hooper	super	_____

USER /usɚ/—final

juicer	looser	_____

UTER /utɚ/—final

bruiter	neuter	shooter
cooter	rooter	suitor
hooter	router	tooter
looter	scooter	tutor

USTER /ustɚ/—final

booster	_____	_____
rooster	_____	_____

UTHER /uðɚ/—final

smoother	soother	_____

UVER /uvɚ/—final

groover	mover	_____
louver	prover	_____

UNYER /unjɚ/—final

junior	_____	_____

UZER /uzɚ/—final

bruiser	cruiser	snoozer
chooser	loser	_____

YUER /juɚ/—final

ewer	mewer	spewer
fewer	newer	viewer
hewer	skewer	_____

YUBER /jubɚ/—final

cuber	_____	_____
tuber	_____	_____

YUCHER /jutʃɚ/—final

future	_____	_____

YUJER /judʒɚ/—final

huger	_____	_____

ER

YUGLER /juglɚ/—**final**
bugler

YUMER /jumɚ/—**final**
fumer   humor   tumor

YUNER /junɚ/—**final**
tuner

YUPER /jupɚ/—**final**
duper
stupor

YUTER /jutɚ/—**final**
cuter   pewter
neuter   tutor

YUZER /juzɚ/—**final**
muser

UCHER /ʊtʃɚ/—**final**
butcher

UFER /ʊfɚ/—**final**
hoofer   roofer   woofer

UGER /ʊgɚ/—**final**
sugar

UKER /ʊkɚ/—**final**
booker   cooker   looker

ULER /ʊlɚ/—**final**
fuller   puller   wooler

UMER /ʊmɚ/—**final**
roomer

UPER /ʊpɚ/—**final**
hooper

USHER /ʊʃɚ/—**final**
busher

UTER /ʊtɚ/—**final**
footer   rooter

UBER /ʌbɚ/—**final**
blubber   grubber   snubber
clubber   rubber   stubber
dubber   scrubber   tubber
drubber   slubber

UMBER /ʌmbɚ/—**final**
cumber   number   umber
lumber   slumber

UCHER /ʌtʃɚ/—**final**
scutcher   toucher

UKCHER /ʌktʃɚ/—**final**
structure

ULCHER /ʌltʃɚ/—**final**
culture   mulcher   vulture

ULPCHER /ʌlptʃɚ/—**final**
sculpture

UNCHER /ʌntʃɚ/—**final**
cruncher   muncher
luncher   puncher

UNKCHER /ʌŋktʃɚ/—**final**
juncture   puncture

ER

UPCHER /ʌptʃɚ/—final
rupture

UDER /ʌdɚ/—final

budder	rudder	udder
flooder	shudder	
mudder	spudder	

UNDER /ʌndɚ/—final

blunder	sunder	under
plunder	thunder	wonder

UFER /ʌfɚ/—final

bluffer	puffer	suffer
buffer	rougher	tougher
fluffer	snuffer	
gruffer	stuffer	

ULFER /ʌlfɚ/—final
sulfur

UGER /ʌgɚ/—final

bugger	lugger	smugger
chugger	plugger	snugger
hugger	slugger	tugger

UJER /ʌdʒɚ/—final

budger	grudger	nudger
drudger	judger	trudger

UNJER /ʌndʒɚ/—final

lunger	plunger	sponger

UKER /ʌkɚ/—final

bucker	pucker	trucker
ducker	shucker	tucker
plucker	sucker	

ULKER /ʌlkɚ/—**final**

skulker	sulker	_____

USKER /ʌskɚ/—**final**

husker	tusker	_____

ULER /ʌlɚ/—**final**

color	duller	sculler
cruller	huller	_____
culler	muller	_____

UBLER /ʌblɚ/—**final**

bubbler	doubler	troubler

UMBLER /ʌmblɚ/—**final**

fumbler	jumbler	stumbler
grumbler	mumbler	tumbler
humbler	rumbler	_____

UDLER /ʌdlɚ/—**final**

buddler	muddler	_____
huddler	puddler	_____

UNDLER /ʌndlɚ/—**final**

bundler	_____	_____
trundler	_____	_____

UFLER /ʌflɚ/—**final**

muffler	scuffler	snuffler
ruffler	shuffler	_____

UGLER /ʌglɚ/—**final**

juggler	smuggler	struggler

UKLER /ʌklɚ/—**final**

buckler	knuckler	truckler
chuckler	suckler	_____

ER

UPLER /ʌpləˑ/—final

coupler	suppler	_____

USLER /ʌsləˑ/—final

bustler	hustler	rustler

UTLER /ʌtləˑ/—final

butler	cutler	sutler

UZLER /ʌzləˑ/—final

guzzler	muzzler	puzzler

UMER /ʌməˑ/—final

bummer	grummer	slummer
comer	hummer	strummer
crumber	mummer	summer
drummer	number	thrummer
glummer	plumber	thumber

UNER /ʌnəˑ/—final

runner	shunner	stunner

UNGGER /ʌŋgəˑ/—final

hunger	_____	_____
younger	_____	_____

UNKER /ʌŋkəˑ/—final

bunker	funker	plunker
clunker	hunker	_____
dunker	junker	_____

UPER /ʌpəˑ/—final

crupper	scupper	supper

UMPER /ʌmpɚ/—final

bumper	plumper	thumper
dumper	pumper	_____
jumper	stumper	_____

USER /ʌsɚ/—final

fusser	_____	_____

ULSER /ʌlsɚ/—final

ulcer	_____	_____

USHER /ʌʃɚ/—final

blusher	flusher	plusher
brusher	gusher	rusher
crusher	musher	usher

UTER /ʌtɚ/—final

butter	mutter	strutter
clutter	putter	stutter
cutter	shutter	utter
flutter	splutter	_____
gutter	sputter	_____

UNTER /ʌntɚ/—final

blunter	hunter	shunter
grunter	punter	_____

USTER /ʌstɚ/—final

bluster	duster	muster
buster	fluster	thruster
cluster	luster	truster

UKSTER /ʌkstɚ/—final

huckster	_____	_____

UNSTER /ʌnstɚ/—final

punster	funster	_____

ER

UNGSTER /ʌŋstɚ/—final
youngster   _____   _____

UTHER /ʌðɚ/—final

brother	other	_____
mother	smother	_____

UVER /ʌvɚ/—final

cover	hover	shover
glover	lover	_____

UZER /ʌzɚ/—final
buzzer   _____   _____

AIRER /ɛərɚ/—final

barer	rarer	starer
bearer	scarer	tearer
carer	sharer	wearer
darer	snarer	where're
fairer	sparer	yarer
parer	squarer	_____

AIRSER /ɛərsɚ/—final
scarcer   _____   _____

ARBER /ɑrbɚ/—final

arbor	barber	harbor

ARCHER /ɑrtʃɚ/—final

archer	larcher	marcher

ARDER /ɑrdɚ/—final

ardor	guarder	larder
carder	harder	_____

ARJER /ɑrdʒɚ/—final

charger	larger	_____

ARKER /ɑrkɚ/—final

barker	marker	starker
darker	parker	_____
larker	sparker	_____

ARKLER /ɑrklɚ/—final

sparkler	_____	_____

ARLER /ɑrlɚ/—final

parlor	snarler	_____

ARBLER /ɑrblɚ/—final

garbler	marbler	_____

ARMER /ɑrmɚ/—final

armor	farmer	_____
charmer	harmer	_____

ARNER /ɑrnɚ/—final

darner	garner	yarner

ARTNER /ɑrtnɚ/—final

partner	_____	_____

ARPER /ɑrpɚ/—final

carper	harper	sharper

ARSER /ɑrsɚ/—final

parser	sparser	_____

ARSHER /ɑrʃɚ/—final

harsher	_____	_____

ER

ARTER /ɑrtɚ/—final

barter	darter	smarter
carter	garter	starter
charter	martyr	tarter

ARTHER /ɑrðɚ/ **—final**
farther

ARVER /ɑrvɚ/ **—final**
carver

ERER /irɚ/ **—final**

cheerer	jeerer	smearer
clearer	nearer	sneerer
dearer	shearer	spearer
hearer	sheerer	steerer

ERDER /irdɚ/ **—final**
weirder

ERSER /irsɚ/ **—final**
fiercer   piercer

IRER /aɪrɚ/ **—final**
direr   hirer   wirer

ORER /ɔrɚ/ **—final**

borer	pourer	soarer
corer	roarer	sorer
floorer	scorer	storer
horror	snorer	

ORCHER /ɔrtʃɚ/ **—final**
scorcher   torture

ORDER /ɔrdɚ/ **—final**

boarder	corder	order
border	hoarder	warder

ORJER /ɔrdʒɚ/ **—final**
forger
gorger

ORKER /ɔrkɚ/—final

corker   porker   _____

ORBLER /ɔrblɚ/—final

warbler   _____   _____

ORMER /ɔrmɚ/—final

dormer   swarmer   _____
former   warmer   _____

ORNER /ɔrnɚ/—final

corner   scorner   _____
mourner   warner   _____

ORPER /ɔrpɚ/—final

torpor   warper   _____

ORSER /ɔrsɚ/—final

coarser   forcer   _____
courser   hoarser   _____

ORTER /ɔrtɚ/—final

mortar   quarter   sorter
porter   shorter   sporter

ORTHER /ɔrðɚ/—final

norther   _____   _____

OURER /aʊrɚ/—final

scourer   sourer   _____

ER

URER /ʊrɚ/—final

juror   poorer   _____
lurer   surer   _____

YURER /jurɚ/—final

curer   purer   furor

URCHER /ɜtʃɚ/—final

lurcher	percher	_____
nurture	searcher	_____

URDER /ɜdɚ/—final

birder	herder	_____
girder	murder	_____

URFER /ɜfɚ/—final

surfer	_____	_____

URGER /ɜgɚ/—final

burger	_____	_____

URJER /ɜdʒɚ/—final

merger	scourger	verger
perjure	urger	_____

URKER /ɜkɚ/—final

jerker	shirker	worker
lurker	smirker	_____

URLER /ɜlɚ/—final

birler	furler	twirler
burler	hurler	whirler
curler	pearler	_____

URDLER /ɜdlɚ/—final

curdler	girdler	hurdler

URMER /ɜmɚ/—final

firmer	murmur	squirmer

URNER /ɜnɚ/—final

burner	learner	turner
churner	spurner	yearner
earner	sterner	

URPER /ɝpɚ/—**final**
chirper _____ _____

URRER /ɝrɚ/—**final**
spurrer stirrer _____

URSER /ɝsɚ/—**final**
bursar nurser terser
cursor purser _____

URTER /ɝtɚ/—**final**
curter hurter spurter
flirter perter squirter

URSTER /ɝstɚ/—**final**
burster _____ _____

URTHER /ɝðɚ/—**final**
further _____ _____

URVER /ɝvɚ/—**final**
fervor server swerver

ER

Also by Valeda D. Blockcolsky, M.S., CCC-SLP . . .

40,000 SELECTED WORDS
Organized by Letter, Sound, and Syllable
with Joan M. Frazer, M.S., CCC-SLP, and Douglas H. Frazer, B.A., J.D.
This outstanding reference is a must for every communication professional in school, hospital, clinic, or office setting. Use it for teaching consonant sounds to all your clients. It's an excellent reference at the university level as well. This alphabetical dictionary groups consonant sounds by initial, medial, and final positions and by consonant clusters/blends. You'll find medial and final sounds and blends not easily found in a standard dictionary, arranged by number of syllables (1 to 6) in each word.

Hardbound edition, Catalog No. 2403-Y	$21.95
Softbound edition, Catalog No. 2300-Y	$19.95
Software version, Catalog No. 7608-Y	$99

Try these additional articulation therapy materials . . .

SPEECHAROO
A Matrix Game for Articulation and Carryover
by Linda M. Fasullo, M.S., CCC-SLP
Encourage carryover of articulation therapy into everyday language. Teach students to pronounce and use target phonemes (/s/, /z/, /l/, and /r/ in all positions; /th/ initial position, voiced and voiceless; /s/ and consonant blends in initial and medial positions) by providing questions for answers in this motivating game. Reinforce everyday use of target sounds in a fun, pragmatic setting. The entertaining format offers a wide variety of subjects for all your students' interests.   **Catalog No. 7757-Y $49**

SPEECH SOUND TRIVIA
For /r/, /s/, and /th/ Articulation Practice
by Karen Dolfi Vargo, M.S.Ed., and Susan Ann Dorsch, B.S.Ed.
A new way for your intermediate and high school students to practice and correctly use /r/, /s/, and /th/ (voiced and unvoiced) in initial and final positions in words. Students read questions from card decks containing words with specific target sounds. As they answer appropriately, they advance their tokens around the gameboard. With reproducible activity sheets to add even more variety to the game.   **Catalog No. 7365-Y $39**

MORE SPEECH SOUND TRIVIA
Articulation Practice for /ch/, /j/, /l/, /r/, and /sh/
by Karen Dolfi Vargo, M.S.Ed., and Susan Ann Dorsch, B.S.Ed.
Target sounds /l/, /sh/, /j/, and /ch/ in initial and final positions and /r/ in medial position with this fun trivia game. You'll have Word Lists, Word Searches, Word Unscramble, Fill-In, and Trivia Challenge for additional pre-practice and carryover assignments. Ideal for use in regular classroom or therapy settings.
                                       Catalog No. 7611-Y $39

ARTICUGAMES
Motivating Drills and Activities
by Elaine Burke Krassowski, M.S., CCC-SLP

Students begin with the formation of sounds in isolation and progress through syllable, word, phrase, sentence, and conversational levels. Use these materials to help students master target phonemes—/s/, /r/, /l/, th, ch, sh, /k/, and /g/. This imaginative collection of motivational activities includes card and board games, progress awards, and worksheets.

Catalog No. 7672-Y **$69**

CURRIC-ARTIC
Curriculum-Based /s/, /r/, and /l/ Vocabulary Lists for Third, Fourth, and Fifth Grade
by Candace M. Moran, M.Ed.

These three manuals for third, fourth, and fifth grade give you curriculum-based word lists for articulation drill and practice. Each manual gives you word lists in initial, medial, and final positions; in blends in those same positions; and in multiple presentations. You'll also have a word list for enhancing self-esteem and increasing self-awareness.

Set of three manuals, Catalog No. 7148-Y **$39**

PICTURE PERFECT 1
Reproducible Stories and Worksheets for Articulation Practice
by Monica Gustafson

You can teach articulation with cartoon illustrations and thematic stories. These stories and worksheets present target phonemes in all positions—initial, medial, and final—and in blends. All materials are reproducible, so you can provide parents with an easy-to-use home program as well.

Catalog No. 7368-Y **$29.95**

PICTURE PERFECT 2
Reproducible Worksheets for Phonological Practice
by Monica Gustafson

Help your clients practice a full range of phonemes with entertaining, illustrated worksheets. Now you can remediate these phoneme groups: fricatives, plosives, affricates, stops, stridents, glides, labials, and more! Worksheets present a target phoneme by consonant classification and individually in the prevocalic and postvocalic contexts. **Catalog No. 7369-Y** **$29.95**

SILLY "SOUND" STORIES
For Articulation and Carryover
by Marie Amerman Woolf, M.A., CCC-SLP

This collection of 30 sound-weighted stories makes the perfect program for articulation stimulation and carryover of consonants. Use these fun, engaging stories to help your young clients improve sound, alphabet, and letter recognition, visual and auditory discrimination, memory, attention, and vocabulary development. Each story also teaches a lesson or moral theme such as Helping Others, Working Together, and Self-Pity. Use the full-page reproducible illustration for each story as the ideal home carryover tool.

Catalog No. 7785-Y **$29.95**

PHOTO ARTICULATION LIBRARY
by Margaret Schrader, Ph.D., CCC-SLP

You'll have 1,085 full-color photo cards for articulation drill and practice, plus carryover for clients of all ages. The extensive index helps you find cards alphabetically, by sound and word positions, and by secondary words. Reinforce initial, medial, and final sounds with these three sets.

Set 1, Catalog No. 7685-Y	$89
Set 2, Catalog No. 7686-Y	$89
Set 3, Catalog No. 7687-Y	$89
All three sets, Catalog No. 7615-Y	$235

LET'S ARTICULATE
Reproducible Drill Sheets for Therapy and Carryover
by Bonita L. Martin, M.A., CCC-SLP, and Greta C. Momeier, M.Ed.

Photocopy these 388 drill tables as you need them. What a great way for you to save money and individualize your articulation therapy! Specific drills show the target sound in initial, medial, and final positions—at word, phrase, and sentence levels. And you can use these pages with children and adults.

Catalog No. 4646-Y $29.95

MORE LET'S ARTICULATE
Reproducible Drill Sheets for Therapy and Carryover
by Bonita L. Martin, M.A., CCC-SLP, and Greta C. Momeier, M.Ed.

Now you can target even more phonemes with this companion to *Let's Articulate*. Here are 214 more reproducible drill lists to help your students make the transition from two-word phrases to four- and six-word sentences. Specific drills show the target sound in initial, medial, and final positions, with administrative sheets to save you time. **Catalog No. 7341-Y $29.95**

YOU DECIDE
Carryover Articulation Stories for /s/ and /r/
by Kathleen Rose Taylor, M.S.

These read-aloud stories concentrate on target sounds while they deal with real-life issues. Your students practice /s/ and /r/ while they participate in the stories—they choose how a story will end, making decisions for the characters and influencing the story's outcome. Each story evokes a new response from your students, naturally providing a variety of discussion topics and opportunities for spontaneous conversation. Includes seven stories each for /s/ and /r/. **Catalog No. 7387-Y $18.95**

YOU SOLVE IT
Carryover Articulation Stories for /s/ and /r/
by Kathleen Rose Taylor, M.S.

Target the phonemes /s/ and /r/ with 16 reproducible cliffhanger mysteries and problem-solving stories. Each sound-weighted story has been left open-ended for your students to solve in their own way. You'll have guided discussions at the end of each story for comprehension, thinking, and analysis by students. Bridge the gap between structured drill and spontaneous conversation with ease! **Catalog No. 7741-Y $19.95**

ARTICUTALES
Stories, Games, and Activities to Sharpen Articulation Skills for S, R, L, K, and G
by Catherine Cronin Carotta and B. Ruth Hall

Charming reproducible illustrations, gameboards, sequence strips, and other manipulatives invite children to participate in hands-on activities. The story-related exercises are great for articulation drill and effective home carryover.   **Catalog No. 7248-Y $19.95**

ARTICULATION TAKEHOMES
Reproducible Articulation Worksheets for Home and Practice
by Holly Ridge and Beverly Ray

Make carryover easy with this variety of illustrated homework pages! Includes a letter to parents encouraging their participation, recordkeeping forms, progress rewards, and charts—a motivating way to reinforce correct target sound production.   **Catalog No. 7508-Y $13.95**

TAKE HOME GAMES
Motivational Activities for Articulation Carryover (S, R, L)
by Debbie Harrison Wieser, B.A.

Your students can achieve carryover more quickly through these enjoyable home assignments. Each reproducible activity offers extensive articulation drill for /s/, /r/, and /l/, in all positions and in blends. Plus, 192 picture cards for additional reinforcement. You'll find all your students' favorite games creatively adapted for phoneme practice—tic-tac-toe, Lotto, Concentration, penny toss, and more.   **Catalog No. 7012-Y $19.95**

Order Form

Communication Skill Builders ®
3830 E. Bellevue/P.O. Box 42050
Tucson, Arizona 85733
(602) 323-7500

Ship to:

INSTITUTION: _____

NAME: _____

TITLE: _____

ADDRESS: _____

CITY: _____ STATE: _____ ZIP: _____

☐ Please check here if this is a permanent address change.
   If so, what was your previous zip code? _____

Telephone No. _____ ☐ work ☐ home

Payment Options:

☐ Personal check included.

☐ School/Hospital/Clinic purchase order enclosed. P.O.# _____

☐ Charge to my credit card.
   ☐ VISA   ☐ MasterCard   ☐ Discover

Card No. ☐☐☐☐☐☐☐☐☐☐☐☐☐☐☐☐☐☐

Expiration Date: Month_____ Year_____

Signature _____

Qty.	Cat. #	Title	Per	Amount
		SUBTOTAL		

Please add 10% for shipping and handling. 8% for orders over $500.
Arizona residents add sales tax.
Canada: Add 22% to subtotal for shipping, handling, and G.S.T.

Payment in U.S. funds only	**TOTAL**

MONEY-BACK GUARANTEE
Upon receipt, you'll have 90 days of risk-free evaluation. If you're not completely satisfied, return your order within 90 days for a full refund of the purchase price. *No Questions Asked!*

FOR PHONE ORDERS
Call (602) 323-7500. Please have your credit card and/or institutional purchase order information ready.
Monday–Friday 9 AM–5 PM,
Saturday 8 AM–2 PM MST / Voice or TDD
FAX (602) 325-0306

We occasionally backorder items temporarily out of stock. If you do not accept backorders, please advise on your purchase order or on this form.